THE OFFICIAL  GUIDE

GRAND PRIX 2005>>

Thumbs-up all round as Michael Schumacher celebrates victory in the 2004 Japanese Grand Prix at Suzuka with the rest of the Ferrari crew

THIS IS A CARLTON BOOK
This edition published in 2005
10 9 8 7 6 5 4 3 2 1

Text and design copyright © Carlton Books Limited 2005

A CIP catalogue record for this book is available from the British Library.

The publisher has taken reasonable steps to check the accuracy of the facts contained herein at the time of going to press but can take no responsibility for any errors.

ISBN 1 84442 578 9

Project Editor: Nigel Matheson
Project Art Direction: Zoë Dissell
Designer: Jim Lockwood
Production: Lisa French
Picture Research: Tom Wright

Printed in the UK

THE OFFICIAL  GUIDE

GRAND PRIX 2005 »

BRUCE JONES

CARLTON
BOOKS

A Gulf Air Airbus salutes the arrival of Formula One in the
Middle East at the inaugural Bahrain Grand Prix, 2004

CONTENTS

The season is almost under starter's orders. The five red lights are about to be lit and then extinguished to release the pack of cars for the first time once more. One burning question remains. Have any of the teams raised their game sufficiently to put one over on reigning champions Ferrari?

Anyone who witnessed last season's final grand prix in Brazil will be fully aware of how exciting Formula One can be. The cars look good, sound great and go like stink, cornering like nothing else on earth and representing the pinnacle of automotive engineering. The drivers are at the peak of their craft. Yes, Michael Schumacher won 13 of last year's grands prix in his Ferrari, but that is very unlikely to happen again.

With the adoption of a new set of technical regulations, there's every reason to be encouraged that BAR, Renault or the resurgent men from Williams and McLaren may be able to step in to the breach and tackle the men in red. It's a case of new season, new rules and a new start – a new roll of the dice for all of the protagonists.

In truth, it would be good for Formula One if Ferrari was to stumble a little in the season ahead, because an all-but-endless string of wins for Schumacher and the Italian team could have people looking for other activities every second Sunday from spring until autumn. Formula One ringmaster Bernie Ecclestone talks of the excitement of witnessing history taking place as Schumacher continues to add to his tally of records, but that last-round battle in Brazil between Williams racer Juan Pablo Montoya and McLaren's Kimi Raikkonen was far more gripping than yet another Ferrari one-two. It was racing, pure and simple.

Look at the main players: Ferrari has hung on to its squad, with not only drivers Schumacher and Rubens Barrichello staying on for more, but also the entire management team. McLaren has also opted for stability, save for the fact that David Coulthard has been replaced by Juan Pablo Montoya.

ANALYSIS OF THE 2005 SEASON »

Williams, meanwhile, has replaced Montoya and Ralf Schumacher with Mark Webber coming in to lead its attack. Changing both drivers is seldom the best way forward.

BAR were delighted to have held on to Jenson Button for 2005 and will be hoping that he and Takuma Sato can guide them to their first win after such a strong campaign last year. Renault also had a great season, outdoing BAR by scoring a win, but being edged out in the battle for second place in the constructors' championship. Their driver pairing of Fernando Alonso and Giancarlo Fisichella will deliver every point their cars are capable of achieving, so it could be Renault's best season since 2002.

Talking of engines, the rule changes mean that the engine manufacturers must now field engines that last for a minimum of two grands prix rather than last year's limit of one. So, expect to see drivers being sent ten places back down the grid as their engines are found wanting and have to be replaced. That will only add to the excitement.

Sauber could well gather a few more points as they start to enjoy the fruits of their wind tunnel for the first time, but budgetary constraints will always prevent the Swiss team from advancing beyond the midfield. Toyota's hierarchy expressed its disappointment at the team's performance last year, when it gathered only nine points. You can be sure that technical director Mike Gascoyne will have produced a superior car, that the engine will be more powerful and that the drivers – Ralf Schumacher and Jarno Trulli – will be better than any that they've had in their three seasons in Formula One so far. Late last year, major moves were made by the team bosses to cut costs; something this is clearly essential as we saw the sad sight of Ford pulling the plug on Jaguar Racing, which has been saved to return as Red Bull Racing. They survived but their near demise sent alarm bells ringing amongst the privateer teams, Jordan and Minardi. Theirs will always be a battle for survival; each year they continue is a success in itself, but they must go on for the sake of the sport, as they are the teams that provide a human face to this mixture of top-line sport and big business.

Encouragingly, there are two new teams gearing up to make their debut in 2006. These are Team Dubai F1, which plans to use chassis and expertise from McLaren and engines from Mercedes, and Midland F1, which is financed by Canadian-Russian entrepreneur Alex Shnaider, using cars built by Dallara and run by Formula Three experts Carlin Motorsport.

FERRARI

Although there's a feeling that Williams and McLaren will be back in the chase in 2005, the standards set by Ferrari last year are hard to follow; they didn't come to be top team for the past six years by accident.

You won't see many reports of Ferrari having failed in 2004. After all, their drivers finished first and second in the championship and the team walked away with the constructors' title, with 15 wins from the 18 races.

However, they did fail to meet technical director Ross Brawn's hoped-for tally of 18 out of 18... Still, you've got to aim high.

Having a team packed with individuals of the calibre of Brawn, chief designer Rory Byrne and engine chief Paolo Martinelli, it's not surprising that Ferrari have maintained the winning formula that they rediscovered in the late 1990s. In less than a decade, the team bearing the prancing horse emblem have reshaped themselves under the guidance of Jean Todt from perennial underachievers to the "Manchester United" of racing; they have become a brand that transcends the sport.

Ferrari is now the team that many fans turn to when they discover Formula One, simply because they want to be associated with a winning outfit. The fact that Ferrari continues to build gorgeous road cars, ones after which the fans can lust, doesn't hurt either, but it's very much a secondary factor in the legions of Ferrari supporters these days, quite the reverse of the way that it was in the 1960s.

The red cars are always very well balanced – on specially developed Bridgestone tyres – fast and,

Rhapsody in red: the Ferrari team gathers round champion Michael Schumacher to celebrate his seventh title

above all, reliable. The pit work is immaculate and their race strategy is among the best. For example, the four-stop tactic Schumacher used to win the French GP bore the mark of genius. Combine that with the unparalleled driving skill of Schumacher and the frequently excellent Rubens Barrichello and it's a daunting challenge for even the best of the opposition. Ferrari's challengers can only hope that the Italian outfit trips up over the new technical regs. But you can rest assured that they won't.

Last year, Ferrari's F2004 surprised its rivals when it was launched because the car didn't look that different to the one that had edged them out in the 2003 title chase. There was no stated change of direction in an attempt to find a quantum leap forward,

THE VIPS

JEAN TODT

Small in stature he may be, but Jean Todt is a giant of management who turned around a fractured team when he took over in 1993. And how: the constructors' title was theirs in 1999 and has remained so ever since, with Michael Schumacher winning the divers' title every year from 2000. Having honed his competitive instincts as a rally co-driver, the Frenchman turned to management with the Peugeot rally team in the mid-1980s and was equally successful.

RORY BYRNE

Seldom seen at a grand prix, designer Rory Byrne is content to weave his magic back at Maranello. The South African came to the UK in 1973 to help a friend in Formula Ford. Having worked as chief designer for Royale Racing Cars from 1974 to '77, Rory moved to Toleman and stayed on when it became Benetton. It was during his time with Benetton that he started his relationship with Michael Schumacher. After joining him at Ferrari in 1997, he has designed every one of the German's title-winning cars. He's booked to stay until the start of 2007.

just a refinement of every part of the F2003-GA's winning equation. The Ferraris pitched up at the season's opening race and dominated it with an imposing one-two finish. Then, as the new Bridgestones came into their own and kept on improving, Ferrari simply moved into a class of its own. The car's reliability was, as ever, exemplary; the mechanical failures that are an accepted part of racing for the other teams are simply not countenanced by the men from Maranello.

Based on last year's evidence, if Ferrari can find a similar improvement this time round and, more importantly, if they can find a way of getting the car off the line better – they were often passed by the Renaults in 2004 – then the best of the rest will find themselves clutching at straws once again.

Ferrari will be using its 2004 car, updated to the new tech spec – with 25 per cent less downforce – for the first four races before introducing its definitive 2005 challenger.

During the close season it was thought that the 2005 engine will be a simple adaptation of its 2004 predecessor, the 053, even though the engine's life must now double from being able to last for an entire grand prix meeting to having to survive for two. To ensure that Ferrari is fully up to speed with the new technical regulations, Marc Gene, after a useful tour of duty at Williams, has been signed up to join its test team alongside Luca Badoer.

For every fan that Ferrari has, and they are there at every grand prix in their tens of thousands, no matter where it's held, the team does have its detractors, with many feeling that they are the FIA's favoured team. Indeed, claims were made last summer that the FIA had been colluding with the Italian outfit over future technical changes. But these stories remain unproven.

However, more opprobrium was heaped upon Ferrari at last year's Brazilian GP when Jean Todt was the odd man out among the ten team bosses; he was the only one who didn't sign up for a set of tech changes that the other bosses thought would help keep costs in check. This had nothing to do with imagined FIA favouritism, but a lot to do with the team trying to ensure their continued position of dominance through extensive testing. It's also safe to say that Fiat president, Luca di Montezemolo, is not the FIA's favourite after he threatened to pull his team out of Formula One following wranglings with Bernie Ecclestone over the division of the sport's income.

FOR THE RECORD

Country of origin:	Italy
Team base:	Maranello, Italy
Telephone:	(39) 0536 949111
Website:	www.ferrari.it
Active in Formula One:	From 1950
Grands Prix contested:	704
Wins:	182
Pole positions:	178
Fastest laps:	181

2004 DRIVERS + RESULTS

Driver	Nationality	Races	Wins	Pts	Pos
Rubens Barrichello	Brazilian	18	2	114	2nd
Michael Schumacher	German	18	13	148	1st

THE TEAM

President:	Luca di Montezemolo
Team principal:	Jean Todt
Technical director:	Ross Brawn
Engine director:	Paolo Martinelli
Team manager:	Stefano Domenicali
Chief designer:	Rory Byrne
Chief engineer:	Luca Baldisserri
Test drivers:	Luca Badoer and Marc Gene
Chassis:	Ferrari F2005
Engine:	Ferrari V10
Tyres:	Bridgestone

The cornerstone of Ferrari's success, Jean Todt at the Australian GP in 2004

MICHAEL SCHUMACHER

There are few superlatives left with which to anoint Michael. Despite having seven Formula One titles in the bag, he is still as keen as mustard to win more. With the best car at his disposal, it's no wonder he keeps winning.

It's hard to know what the future holds for Michael. If he could have it his own way, he'd keep on racing until he drops and, with his supreme level of fitness, that could be well into his nineties. You might be churlish and point to his scratchy form in last year's Chinese and Brazilian GPs, but as the title was already in the bag, he could be forgiven for taking his eye off the ball for just a fraction. The sight of him spinning in both races might just act as a spur, though, to those lining up in the hope of replacing him at the top of the tree.

With rule changes in place for 2005, it may well be that Ferrari's level of competitiveness is not what it was last year. Indeed, had it not been for his clash with Montoya in the tunnel during last year's Monaco GP, Michael could have won the first 13 grands prix – a feat that would have shattered Alberto Ascari's record of nine consecutive wins.

With Ferrari opting for the status quo again by keeping its entire management structure and Rubens Barrichello as his team-mate, Michael has every reason to feel comfortable with his environment. He will, no doubt, have every intention of keeping those wins flowing and cocking a snook at those who say that his continued domination is a blight on F1.

TRACK NOTES

Nationality:	**GERMAN**
Born:	**3 JANUARY, 1969, KERPEN, GERMANY**
Website:	**www.michael-schumacher.de**
Teams:	**JORDAN 1991, BENETTON 1991–1995, FERRARI 1996–2005**
First Grand Prix:	**1991 BELGIAN GP**
Grand Prix starts:	**213**
Grand Prix wins:	**83**

1992 Belgian GP, **1993** Portuguese GP, **1994** Brazilian GP, Pacific GP, San Marino GP, Monaco GP, Canadian GP, French GP, Hungarian GP, European GP, **1995** Brazilian GP, Spanish GP, Monaco GP, French GP, German GP, Belgian GP, European GP, Pacific GP, Japanese GP, **1996** Spanish GP, Belgian GP, Italian GP, **1997** Monaco GP, Canadian GP, French GP, Belgian GP, Japanese GP, **1998** Argentinian GP, Canadian GP, French GP, British GP, Hungarian GP, Italian GP, **1999** San Marino GP, Monaco GP, **2000** Australian GP, Brazilian GP, San Marino GP, European GP, Canadian GP, Italian GP, US GP, Japanese GP, Malaysian GP, **2001** Australian GP, Malaysian GP, Spanish GP, Monaco GP, European GP, French GP, Hungarian GP, Belgian GP, Japanese GP, **2002** Australian GP, Brazilian GP, San Marino GP, Spanish GP, Austrian GP, Canadian GP, British GP, French GP, German GP, Belgian GP, Japanese GP, **2003** San Marino GP, Spanish GP, Austrian GP, Canadian GP, Italian GP, US GP, **2004** Australian GP, Malaysian GP, Bahrain GP, San Marino GP, Spanish GP, European GP, Canadian GP, US GP, French GP, British GP, German GP, Hungarian GP, Japanese GP

Poles:	**63**
Fastest laps:	**65**
Points:	**1186**
Honours:	**2004, 2003, 2002, 2001, 2000, 1995 & 1994 FORMULA ONE CHAMPION, 1998 FORMULA ONE RUNNER-UP, 1990 GERMAN FORMULA THREE CHAMPION & MACAU GP WINNER, 1988 GERMAN FORMULA KONIG CHAMPION**

You can be sure of Schumacher, as he's not a driver who loses his focus. Expect more wins...

TURNING POINT

It was blitzkrieg for Germany's young stars from the instant that Michael stepped up from karts in 1988. He was pipped to the 1989 Formula Three title by Karl Wendlinger. He dominated in 1990, but was put in his place in the final round by a visitor, Mika Hakkinen. Michael was determined to gain revenge in the end-of-season thrash around the streets of Macau. But he was beaten by the Finn in the first heat. Hakkinen could afford to finish behind Michael in the second heat and still take outright victory on aggregate times, as long as he finished close enough to the German. Leading going into the final lap, Hakkinen had it in the bag, but the pair touched and the Finn was out on the spot. Michael limped around to the finish to claim the jewel in F3's crown.

RUBENS BARRICHELLO

Team-mate to Michael Schumacher for the sixth season, Rubens will be out for more wins this time around and might even have a crack at winning his home GP. Going for the title, however, is out of the question.

Rubens Barrichello, the man who is happy to play second fiddle to first violinist Michael Schumacher

Rubens once said that winning his home race would mean more to him than winning the F1 world championship. Well, consider Rubens' 2004 record next to that of his dominant team-mate Michael Schumacher and it's clear to see why this affable Brazilian is likely to be shooting for the former this year rather than the latter. His 2004 tally was two wins to Michael's 13 and Rubens was outqualified by the German in 13 of the 18 grands prix. It's not a record that is likely to swing the team behind him rather than Michael. Then again, the whole team is built around Michael and that's that. Providing that Ferrari doesn't trip up over the new technical regulations, Rubens will have every chance of adding more grand prix wins to his tally. But while Michael remains as his team-mate, claiming the world title is likely to remain beyond his grasp.

TURNING POINT

Everything seemed to go right for Rubens as he bagged his national karting series in 1988 and then the Formula Opel Euroseries in 1990, his first year in Europe. Then came British Formula Three in 1991. This was the toughest of all F3 series, the one that had launched, among others, Ayrton Senna. Hoping to emulate his compatriot, Rubens signed for the same team, West Surrey Racing, and started the season as title favourite. Qualifying on pole was to become his forte, getting away well off the line his Achilles heel. The season turned into a battle between Rubens, David Coulthard and Gil de Ferran. The win that turned it around came at Donington Park, when he led all the way from pole while Coulthard could finish only fourth and de Ferran fifth. He took another win in the following round which meant he nicked the title from Coulthard.

Given all of that, however, the failure to win his home grand prix will have haunted Rubens all winter. He arrived at his home track of Interlagos last year with the unbelievably poor record of ten retirements from 11 visits, several times after leading. This time he started from pole and Michael from 18th, but it still didn't come together as the changing track conditions left him struggling for grip and he ended up third.

Still, at least Rubens netted a pair of wins. While the first of these, at Monza, was a surprise result as he and Michael came on in the latter stages as if powered by rockets to overhaul Jenson Button's BAR, his victory at the inaugural Chinese GP will have given him particular pleasure, as his will always be the first name on the list of winners at the Shanghai circuit.

BAR

BAR came of age in 2004, vaulting past long-established teams to be the best of the rest behind Ferrari.

Having held on to the services of Jenson Button for 2005, they will be going all out to land that first race win.

Takuma Sato (above) and Jenson Button are back for more, both gunning for that all-important first win for BAR with increased input from Honda

Ex-team principal David Richards spent the latter part of last summer fuming about the fact that the contract he thought had tied Jenson Button to the team for 2005 could be considered anything less than binding. Lawyers for Williams thought the contract contained a loophole that could lead to Button becoming a free agent and they tried to lure him back to their fold. The matter was put in front of the Contract Recognition Board, and the situation was finally sorted. Button is staying with BAR.

While this was the outcome sought by BAR, it became an unnecessary distraction, delaying their development programme for 2005. Although members of the team, such as technical director Geoff Willis, left the legal wranglings to Richards, it undoubtedly

had an effect on the entire outfit. Then, late in November, Richards handed the reins to managing director Nick Fry, who will run the team as Richards departs to concentrate on his Prodrive competition engineering empire.

The wrangling also took the spotlight away from what was BAR's best season by far. Finally the most stylish team in the paddock was hitting the heights that team founders Adrian Reynard and Craig Pollock had promised when they started in 1999.

The fact that Button was regularly the best of the rest behind the Ferrari drivers and that he was also challenging for the team's first win will not have been lost on Jacques Villeneuve who spent five years trying to attain such a level of competitiveness before leaving the

THE VIPS

NICK FRY
The departure of David Richards has opened the door for Nick to lead the BAR team. A career motor industry man, Nick gained experience with Ford and then Richards' Prodrive motorsport engineering empire before being seconded to support Richards as managing director at BAR. Principle team investor Honda liked what he did in sorting out the team's internal structure and were more than happy when he stepped up at the end of 2004 to lead the team.

GEOFF WILLIS
Geoff took the unusual route to motor racing via designing yachts for the Americas Cup. Having joined the Leyton House team in 1990, Geoff made quite an impact by introducing Computational Fluid Dynamics, a concept that all other designers have since harnessed. Williams snapped him up for his CFD skills and Geoff became chief aerodynamicist. He took over joint care of the designs with Gavin Fisher in 1997 once Adrian Newey left and then joined BAR for 2002 as technical director, giving him overall control of the entire design side.

One day all this will be yours - Dave Richards has a word in Nick Fry's ear

in the San Marino GP set the tone. As did his unrewarded pursuit of Jarno Trulli in Monaco. However, it was Button's climb from 13th on the grid to second in the German GP that stood out. Even Michael Schumacher was shocked by his pace that day. Sato had his moments too, occasionally outpacing his team-mate, and his joy at being on the podium at the US GP is sure to have fired up a whole new generation of Japanese fans. It will also have strengthened the resolve of Honda to take more of a role with the team, something that was shown last November when they increased their stake in BAR to 45% and put up money for a £30m wind tunnel.

With both Button and Sato staying on for 2005, their form can only improve. The important thing is whether BAR will continue to improve the competitiveness of their cars with a lightweight carbon gearbox or whether sleeping giants McLaren and Williams will overhaul them and prevent Button and Sato from winning.

team at the end of the 2003 season.

Rival teams were also left with a sneer on their faces at the start of last year. They assumed that the 006's form in pre-season testing was down to running with light fuel loads in order to set quick lap times to impress sponsors.

When the racing got under way, it was clear that they had underestimated the first BAR car to have been produced with a full input from Willis and the team vaulted past Williams, McLaren and Renault as the outfit most capable of taking the battle to Ferrari. By season's end, the drivers had visited the podium 11 times – Button ten times and Sato once – but still had to occupy the top step as Ferrari's drivers dominated. Perhaps all this will change in the season ahead.

It wasn't just the work that Willis and his design and engineering team had done in penning such an effective chassis that made the 006 work, it was also BAR's switch to Michelin rubber which was clearly better than the Bridgestones that had been made just to suit Ferrari in 2003. Engine supplier and partner Honda also deserve much credit for the V10 that they built, as it was both smaller than before and, helpfully, had a lower centre of gravity. It also pushed out more power, with the engines that Honda brought out for their home race at Suzuka said to produce 960bhp.

There were complaints about the legality of BAR's Front Torque Transfer braking system and so this had to be simplified. Indeed, BAR has agreed to drop its special front diff for 2005. BAR was also hit by the banning of flexi wings in late summer, but this showed how hard they'd been pushing to find any advantage they could to overhaul Renault to rank second overall in the constructors' championship.

Picking out a few highlights is hard to do as there were so many, but Button's pole and second place

FOR THE RECORD

Country of origin:	England
Team base:	Brackley, England
Telephone:	(44) 01280 844000
Website:	www.BARf1.com
Active in Formula One:	From 1999
Grands Prix contested:	101
Wins:	0
Pole positions:	1
Fastest laps:	0

2004 DRIVERS + RESULTS

Driver	Nationality	Races	Wins	Pts	Pos
Jenson Button	**British**	18	-	85	3rd
Takuma Sato	**Japanese**	18	-	34	8th

THE TEAM

Team principal:	**Nick Fry**
Technical director:	**Geoff Willis**
Chief designers:	**Joerg Zander and Kevin Taylor**
Chief engineer:	**Craig Wilson**
Team manager:	**Ron Meadows**
Test/Third driver:	**Anthony Davidson**
Chassis:	**BAR 007**
Engine:	**Honda V10**
Tyres:	**Michelin**

JENSON BUTTON

Remove Michael Schumacher from the reckoning and Jenson was the star of last season. Small wonder BAR and Williams fought over his services for 2005. BAR won and Button will be determined to turn them into winners.

Tuned in: Jenson Button found a new focus in 2004 and will be intent on winning in 2005

Jenson has always had promise and his performances last season confirmed this fact after he had had to endure a few seasons in which the machinery at his disposal was poor. People also complained he was too absorbed in a jet-set lifestyle, but lessons have clearly been learned and in 2004 he was mighty. The highlight was his drive from 13th on the grid at the German GP to a fast-closing second behind Michael Schumacher. It certainly gave Michael food for thought.

There's no escaping the fact that Jenson had hoped to be a Williams driver this year and both he and his manager John Byfield made a bid for him to quit BAR ahead of time. This didn't work out, so Jenson will have to wait until 2006 to return to the team that gave him his F1 break.

The announcement that he was planning to leave could have both destabilized his position within the team and stalled BAR's progress. To the credit of all involved, it didn't. This was shown when Jenson raced to the front at the Italian GP and remained there until both Ferraris blasted past with a display of extraordinary late-race speed. That he went on to end the year ranked third overall emphasizes why both teams were fighting so hard for his services.

Jenson's decision to move wasn't based on a desire for greater pay; it was based more on his perception that he stands a better chance of becoming world champion with Williams. Judging by BAR's superiority in 2004, he may well be better-placed where he is for the 2005 season. Then again, the sport's pendulum keeps swinging in the pack of teams trying to topple Ferrari and it won't have escaped people's attention that victory in last year's final round went to Williams.

TRACK NOTES

Nationality:	**BRITISH**
Born:	**19 JANUARY, 1980, FROME, ENGLAND**
Website:	**www.jensonbutton.com**
Teams:	**WILLIAMS 2000, BENETTON/RENAULT 2001-2002, BAR 2003-2005**
First Grand Prix:	**2000 AUSTRALIAN GP**
Grand Prix starts:	84
Grand Prix wins:	0
	best result: second, **2004** San Marino GP, Monaco GP, German GP, Chinese GP
Poles:	1
Fastest laps:	0
Points:	130
Honours:	**1999 MACAU FORMULA THREE RUNNER-UP, 1998 FORMULA FORD FESTIVAL WINNER & BRITISH FORMULA FORD CHAMPION, 1998 McLAREN AUTOSPORT BRDC YOUNG DRIVER, 1997 EUROPEAN SUPER A KART CHAMPION, 1991 BRITISH CADET KART CHAMPION**

TURNING POINT

Everyone who had observed his successes in karts knew Jenson was a talent. Then, when he won the British Formula Ford title and Festival at his first attempt in 1998, even more people paid attention. However, it was Jenson's form in Formula Three in 1999 that was the clincher. On pole for the opening round, he took his first win third time out. High-speed Thruxton is hard to get right, yet Jenson placed his Promatecme Dallara on the outside of the front row then got the jump on pole-sitter Andrew Kirkaldy and fended off his best efforts and those of his Stewart Racing team-mate Luciano Burti. This was all the more impressive, as Jenson's Renault engine wasn't a match for his rivals' Mugens on a circuit where power counts. He didn't win the title, but it proved he was ready for higher things, like a shoot-out for a Williams seat...

TAKUMA SATO

It's safe to say that a nation expects. Following Takuma's maiden visit to the podium last year, the Japanese are looking for him to become Japan's first grand prix winner. To do so at Suzuka would suit them just fine...

National stereotyping is a terrible thing, but Takuma is everything you wouldn't expect from a Japanese driver. He is flamboyant in his driving style and funny rather than steady and humourless. Small wonder, then, that Honda is putting its might behind Takuma and BAR; they are fully aware of the PR possibilities if they could make him the first Japanese driver to win a grand prix. As it is, Japanese papers were filled with eulogistic reports when he achieved his only podium visit thus far, at last year's US GP.

Takuma spent last year in Jenson Button's shadow as the English driver chased after the Ferraris, but it wasn't all one-sided, as their 11-7 qualifying tally (in Button's favour) shows, with Takuma having a strong run mid-season when he was every bit as fast as his team-mate. What he must find for 2005, though, is consistency.

Takuma made his F1 debut, with Jordan in 2002, but people forget that he is lining up for only his third season in the category rather than his fourth. He spent 2003 as BAR's test driver before Honda gave him a ride in place of Jacques Villeneuve. He clearly absorbed the lessons that needed to be learnt - such as continuing at Monaco with an engine that was blowing and gushing oil, then stopping himself from over-driving after a warning from team principal David Richards. A strong run of results towards the end of the season not only moved him up to eighth in the driver rankings but it also helped ensure that BAR ended the year as runner-up to Ferrari in the constructors' championship.

For the sake of racing fans the world over, though, nobody wants Takuma to curb his wilder side too much, as his ability to get out of shape and catch it in the blink of an eye remains one of the most compelling sights in F1.

Takuma Sato will be looking to ally consistency to his undoubted speed in this year's campaign

TURNING POINT

The interesting thing about Takuma's career is that he missed out on karting. Then, rather than trying to find his feet in Japan, Takuma headed for Britain in 1998. By the second half of 1999, he'd stepped up to Formula Three. Graduating to the main class in 2000, he started winning and ranked third behind Antonio Pizzonia and Tomas Scheckter. For 2001, again with Carlin, he was partnered by Anthony Davidson and was to end the year as champion after the battle see-sawed between them. However, the highlight of his year, the race that confirmed his supremacy, was his victory at the Marlboro Masters - an invitation race at the home of the defunct Dutch GP: Zandvoort. Forty-five drivers went out to qualify and Takuma was fastest, albeit then having a huge accident. In the race, though, he simply dominated from Andre Lotterer, who later became a Jaguar test driver. Davidson was third and Gianmaria Bruni fourth.

TRACK NOTES

Nationality:	**JAPANESE**
Born:	**28 JANUARY, 1977, TOKYO, JAPAN**
Website:	**www.takumasato.com**
Teams:	**JORDAN 2002, BAR 2003-2005**
First Grand Prix:	**2002 AUSTRALIAN GP**
Grand Prix starts:	**36**
Grand Prix wins:	**0**
	best result: third **2004** US GP
Poles:	**0**
Fastest laps:	**0**
Points:	**39**
Honours:	**2001 BRITISH FORMULA THREE CHAMPION**

RENAULT

Renault stepped up one place to third overall in 2004, but it could easily have been second. It shows how far the team has come and Fernando Alonso, plus the returning Giancarlo Fisichella, will be out for more wins in 2005.

Spanish fly: this season Fernando Alonso will be going all out to return to the winners' circle for Renault after a fallow 2004 campaign

Don't believe everything you hear on the grapevine: Renault isn't facing its final season in the sport's top category. This rumour gained momentum last autumn, with many reckoning that the arrival of Carlos Ghosn as the new boss of the French manufacturer would lead to the Formula One team being axed to save money. However, Ghosn swiftly allayed such fears and Renault will be racing on until the end of 2007 at the very least.

Ghosn will expect the team to close in for the kill this time around, rather than allow itself to be overhauled in the closing stages as it was last year, when BAR caught up and then pulled clear of Renault to rank as runners-up behind Ferrari. This year will be more competitive, too, as Williams and McLaren are sure to carry on the fine form that saw them head-

ing the field at the final round.

Although there's the upheaval of having to make its engines last for two grands prix rather than one, Renault's engine experts at least have the continuity of engine format for 2005. This will come as a welcome relief, since last year was seen very much as a learning year engine-wise after the team had to scrap its wide vee-angled engines and fight to get its 72-degree V10 up to speed. Team principal Flavio Briatore said that it wouldn't be good until the races in Europe and although Alonso took a podium first time out, albeit well off the pace of the Ferraris, it wasn't quite as ready as expected. In truth, although more powerful than the wide vee engine, it was always short of peak power. Fortunately, it counteracted this by its incredible ability off the line and by its

THE VIPS

FLAVIO BRIATORE
No man walking the paddock has a higher profile than Flavio Briatore. Yet, beneath the playboy image, Flavio is a serious businessman. This has sometimes rankled because he's not a motorsport fan, but his success since being encouraged to take control of the Benetton team in 1989 after helping the Italian knitwear company establish its name in the USA has been impressive. After guiding Michael Schumacher to the drivers' title in 1994 and '95, Flavio set up Supertec to supply Renault's ex-works engines before rejoining the team in 2000.

PAT SYMONDS
Pat is very much one of the old guard. After working for Formula Ford constructors Hawke and Royale, Pat joined Toleman in 1981, later working in the wind tunnel and staying on as a race engineer when the team metamorphosed into Benetton. Having been director of engineering for the stillborn Reynard F1 project, he returned to Benetton, was appointed technical director in 1996 and stayed on as director of engineering when the team changed again, to become Renault, in 2002.

Renault F1 front man, Flavio Briatore caught in an unusually reflective mood

With Trulli having been dropped, Alonso will be joined by Giancarlo Fisichella – who raced for the Benetton team between 1998 and 2001, leaving it a year before it metamorphosed into Renault. Alonso is expected to raise his game after a season that disappointed those who had marvelled at his ascendancy in 2003. However, he was never confident in his car's handling and that played a large part in his below-par performances. Fisichella is sure to deliver as many points as the R25 is capable of, as he remains one of the best racers. Their duel should be well worth watching and they will both have prayed long and hard that technical director Bob Bell and chief engineer Pat Symonds can produce a chassis with all of the attributes of the R24 with better balance and obviously a more competitive engine.

torquey nature: Jarno Trulli was able to harness both when he led from start to finish at Monaco.

Only at season's end were the team's stunning starts attributed to a long gearbox which helps to get weight back over the rear wheels and makes up for the loss of launch control that had been banned for 2004. Unfortunately for Renault, a rule change to negate this advantage was expected over the winter.

The car's handling was of far greater concern than the lack of horsepower. The team had looked at changing to a twin-keel chassis, but rejected the idea because of the drawbacks it would have posed structurally. However, in terms of handling, both drivers found the R24 "difficult". On the plus side, it was faster than its predecessor.

With Ferrari winning almost every race, it was hard for teams such as Renault to get a look in, so it came as quite a surprise that they started hinting that Trulli may be on the way out after his win at Monaco. Then, after his huge accident at the British GP, when his rear suspension is thought to have collapsed, the Italian lost faith in the car, his form suffered and he was dropped for the final three races.

The choice of Trulli's replacement for those final three races caused many a raised eyebrow, though. Instead of promoting trusty test driver Franck Montagny – a Frenchman after all – chief executive Patrick Faure opted for Jacques Villeneuve, a driver who would be racing for Sauber in 2005 and therefore someone who would be able to take the team's secrets with him. That he wasn't fast enough to score the points that Renault so badly needed to challenge BAR in the battle to be runner-up made the choice look all the worse. Former world champion Alain Prost took the team to task and is known to be angling to find a place on its management team, just a few years after the demise of his own team.

For now, Briatore remains at the helm, although his contract is up at the end of this year. Whether it's extended remains to be seen, but the pitlane would be a duller place without the flamboyant Italian.

FOR THE RECORD

Country of origin:	**England**
Team base:	**Enstone, England**
Telephone:	**(44) 01608 678000**
Website:	**www.renaultf1.com**
Active in Formula One:	**From 1977–85 & from 2002**
Grands Prix contested:	**174***
Wins:	**17**
Pole positions:	**36**
Fastest laps:	**19**

* Note these figures don't include the 238 races the team ran as Benetton

2004 DRIVERS + RESULTS

Driver	Nationality	Races	Wins	Pts	Pos
Fernando Alonso	**Spanish**	18	-	59	4th
Jarno Trulli	**Italian**	15	1	46	6th
Jacques Villeneuve	**Canadian**	3	-	-	N/A

THE TEAM

Chairman:	**Patrick Faure**
Managing director:	**Flavio Briatore**
Technical director:	**Bob Bell**
Chief engineer:	**Pat Symonds**
Chief designer:	**Tim Densham**
Sporting manager:	**Steve Nielsen**
Test driver:	**Franck Montagny**
Chassis:	**Renault R25**
Engine:	**Renault V10**
Tyres:	**Michelin**

FERNANDO ALONSO

Having arguably been the star of 2003, last year was tougher, but it was a year of development for both Fernando and the Renault team and the Spaniard is set to come out with all guns blazing in 2005.

Standing on the podium at last year's Australian GP, as the best of the rest behind the Ferrari drivers, Fernando might have thought he was set for a run of results like those he attained in 2003 and, perhaps, he might even have thought that he had a chance of victory should the Ferraris fail. However, the subsequent 17 races yielded just three more visits to the podium and no wins. Yes, the Spaniard climbed from sixth overall in 2003 to fourth last year, but many saw his season as disappointing.

In fairness, this criticism only arose when compared to their high hopes for him, hopes that envisaged him taking on Michael Schumacher at the front end of the field. But no driver who retires from five rounds will ever do that. In truth, it was another season of solid progress for both Fernando and the Renault team and his lack of wins will no doubt spur him to greater things this year.

Fernando will have Giancarlo Fisichella as a team-mate for 2005 rather than friend Jarno

Trulli. This might prove to be a masterstroke as his desire to beat a driver with whom he doesn't have such a strong bond will be all the greater. Whatever occurs, Fernando is a racer par excellence, who comes alive once the red lights go out, not only because of Renault's renowned alacrity off the line but also because he has the ability to drive the entire race as though it's a qualifying lap. When the car allowed him to, he showed this in performances such as the one in Brazil when he started on dry tyres and slid to the back of the field before rocketing through the order to lead. It was a masterful drive - totally different from his pole-to-second-place performance in Renault's home grand prix at Magny-Cours.

A man with the ability to pull out all the stops when needed, Fernando Alonso is a national hero in Spain

TURNING POINT

In a brilliant junior career that saw him landing the world karting title in 1996 at the age of 15 and then graduate to cars in 1999, winning the Formula Nissan title at his first attempt, Fernando really made his mark in 2000. This was in Formula 3000, but he took a while to find the measure of more experienced drivers. He earned his first podium finish for Astromega at the penultimate round at the Hungaroring and then simply blitzed everyone at the toughest track they visited: Spa-Francorchamps. Fernando qualified on pole and was never headed. He left eventual champion Bruno Junqueira in his wake, as well as Justin Wilson and Mark Webber. Only team-mate Marc Goossens, a local expert, stayed anywhere near him, albeit finishing 15s adrift.

TRACK NOTES

Nationality:	**SPANISH**
Born:	**29 JULY, 1981, OVIEDO, SPAIN**
Website:	**www.fernandoalonso.com**
Teams:	**MINARDI 2001,**
	RENAULT 2003-2005
First Grand Prix:	**2001 AUSTRALIAN GP**
Grand Prix starts:	**51**
Grand Prix wins:	**1**
	2003 Hungarian GP
Poles:	**3**
Fastest laps:	**1**
Points:	**104**
Honours:	**1999 FORMULA NISSAN**
	CHAMPION, 1997 ITALIAN & SPANISH
	KART CHAMPION, 1996 WORLD &
	SPANISH KART CHAMPION, 1995 & 1994
	SPANISH JUNIOR KART CHAMPION

GIANCARLO FISICHELLA

Giancarlo has had an on-off relationship with long-time manager Flavio Briatore and, this year, he's back driving for his team, Renault, albeit with Flavio suggesting that he's too lazy to beat team-mate Fernando Alonso...

"Fisi" has no time for politics or histrionics which makes him a very popular figure in the paddock

TRACK NOTES

Nationality:	**ITALIAN**
Born:	**14 JANUARY 1973, ROME, ITALY**
Website:	**www.giancarlofisichella.it**
Teams:	**MINARDI 1996, JORDAN 1997 AND 2002-03, BENETTON 1998-2001, SAUBER 2004, RENAULT 2005**
First Grand Prix:	**1996 AUSTRALIAN GP**
Grand Prix starts:	**142**
Grand Prix wins:	**1**
	2003 Brazilian GP
Poles:	**1**
Fastest laps:	**1**
Points:	**116**

Honours: **1994 ITALIAN FORMULA THREE CHAMPION AND MONACO FORMULA THREE WINNER, 1991 EUROPEAN KART RUNNER-UP, 1990 WORLD KART RUNNER-UP, 1989 EUROPEAN KART RUNNER-UP**

You might think that this is a curious form of "support" from Briatore, but it was probably intended more as a means of motivation, to get his Italian compatriot out of the comfort zone and into a mindset that will have him showing the form that we've seen over the years. There were flashes of brilliance, such as running in second place in Argentina for Jordan in 1997 and leading the German GP that same year, but he has never been at the wheel of superior equipment, and so it's little surprise that Giancarlo didn't win until 2003. Indeed, that he won at all in a Jordan - a midfield car at best that year - is a tribute to his doggedness.

A glance at last year's results shows that he peaked with fourth place in the US GP when Bridgestones were very much the tyre to have, but his best run was probably when he came in fifth in the Belgian GP.

This year, those who admire his talent will get to see how he stacks up against rising star Fernando Alonso, and this will no doubt be a better gauge of his abilities than being compared with erstwhile Sauber team-mate Felipe Massa, who has had only Nick Heidfeld to compare himself against thus far, making it hard to assess his relative ability as the German driver has also spent time with less-than-competitive teams. One thing that Fisi will do well to note is that although he is managed by Briatore, Alonso has the added advantage of being Briatore's favourite.

TURNING POINT

When you're trying to make a name for yourself in the junior categories you have to make sure you win races and titles and hope no one newer and faster comes to spoil the show. This is something that Fisichella, ex-runner-up in the world karting championship, did once he had reached Formula Three, winning the Italian title at his third attempt in 1994. However, it was his win at the Monaco F3 GP that year that saved his career. He couldn't afford to graduate to Formula 3000, so his victory from pole over Germans Jorg Muller and Sascha Maassen around the streets of the principality was his salvation as Alfa Romeo snapped up his services to race in the International Touring Car Championship, a ride that would keep him in the public eye long enough for Minardi to help him into Formula One in 1996. The rest is history...

WILLIAMS

Having won the final race of 2004, Williams might well feel they are ready to challenge Ferrari again.

But there are new technical regulations for 2005 and a brace of new drivers to factor in to the equation.

It's all change at Williams as Ralf Schumacher (above) and Juan Pablo Montoya have moved on, opening the way for Mark Webber to lead the team

It's amazing what a win can do for morale. Take Williams, for example. Winless since the French GP in 2003, all that was forgotten when Juan Pablo Montoya guided them to victory in Brazil over McLaren's Kimi Raikkonen in the final race of 2004, with Ferrari out of touch. Ralf Schumacher also put one over on his older brother at Interlagos, but neither of the Williams drivers have stayed on for the season ahead and have been replaced by Mark Webber and Antonio Pizzonia.

Webber's signing from Jaguar was straightforward, but much of the tail-end of last season for Sir Frank Williams was spent in meetings with lawyers after he had been led to believe that Jenson Button's contract with BAR might not be watertight. Anxious to have him

back on board, Frank's lawyers made a bid. The matter went to the Contract Recognition Board and the outcome was that Button wouldn't be returning to the team after a four-year break after all. Then the rumour mill swung into action and 2004 stand-in Antonio Pizzonia was tipped to fill the seat. Both David Coulthard and Nick Heidfeld pushed hard for the drive. Anthony Davidson was also mentioned in despatches. Then so too was Mika Hakkinen. Eventually, Pizzonia was given the nod.

The other factor that will affect whether this victory can be repeated is the change in technical regulations for 2005, with engine partner BMW having an obvious interest in whether its new engines can prove as competitive as they did in 2004

THE VIPS

SIR FRANK WILLIAMS
There are some in Formula One circles who are driven by the money: Frank Williams is not one of them. He is a racer, pure and simple. Having showed his skill in running Piers Courage in Formula One from 1969, Frank lost his way somewhat, scratching a living until he teamed up with Patrick Head in 1977 to form Williams Grand Prix Engineering. Nine constructors' titles followed, with Jones, Mansell, Prost etc.

SAM MICHAEL
It's just as well the 33-year-old Australian is ambitious because he has a massive pair of boots to fill in replacing Patrick Head as the team's technical chief. Sam joined Lotus in 1994, after graduating as a mechanical engineer. He moved on to Jordan in 1995 and succeeded to such an extent that he ran their R&D side in 1996 and '97. A race engineer between 1998 and 2000, he formed a strong bond with Ralf Schumacher and followed him to Williams in 2001, starting as chief operations engineer before being promoted midway through last year.

now that their life has been forced to extend over two race meetings rather than one.

There are, of course, further factors that may affect their chances: such as the enforced aero changes that have slashed downforce and the fact that a set of tyres must last a whole race. However, what these changes will show is whether technical director Sam Michael has been able to step up to the plate and guide the team through these rule changes in a better way than his peers from rival teams. If he does, then long-time technical leader Patrick Head might even allow himself one of those rare smiles, happy that his succession is starting to work out.

The design process suffered a knock-back last September when chief designer Gavin Fisher was hurt in a motorbike shunt. However, Williams have strength in depth on the design side, with Loic Bigois

taking over as chief aerodynamicist last November when Antonia Terzi quit; the Frenchman will be looking forward to using the team's new wind tunnel that came on stream in April 2004. Terzi wasn't the first to leave, though, as long-standing engineer Tim Preston had already left. He'd stood down from the race team to the less-pressured environment of the test team several years ago before stepping back to help the race outfit, but now he's off. It's up to Michael to guide them in a way that encourages them to produce their best. And, in turn, try not to race with parts that don't comply with the rules, following the embarrassment for Michael at last year's Canadian GP when wrong-sized brake ducts led to the disqualification of both the team's cars.

Success in reading the rule changes better than the others will also help Williams bounce back from when it shocked everyone

last year with the launch of its FW26. Not only had they switched from a single-keel chassis design to a twin-keel, just as twin-keel protagonists Sauber went the other way, but they'd done so in a radical way. With wide-spaced tusks coming down from a short, high nose to the front wing, the car was dubbed "walrus nose". Trouble was, aerodynamicist Terzi's concept didn't appear to work. Indeed, apart from a strong run from Montoya in Malaysia, it was well off the pace

and lacked the downforce needed to give the drivers confidence going into corners. Although Terzi was given a vote of confidence, the "walrus nose" was replaced by a standard nose from the Hungarian GP on. But it took time to convert it into a front-running car, although Ralf Schumacher did a great job on his second race back from injuring his back in the US GP to finish second behind his brother at the Japanese GP. Then, of course, came that win in Brazil.

FOR THE RECORD

Country of origin:	England
Team base:	Grove, England
Telephone:	(44) 01235 777700
Website:	www.bmw.williamsf1.com
Active in Formula One:	From 1973
Grands Prix contested:	496
Wins:	113
Pole positions:	124
Fastest laps:	128

2004 DRIVERS + RESULTS

Driver	Nationality	Races	Wins	Pts	Pos
Marc Gene	Spanish	2	-	-	N/A
Juan Pablo Montoya	Colombian	18	1	58	5th
Antonio Pizzonia	Brazilian	4	-	6	15th
Ralf Schumacher	German	12	-	24	9th

THE TEAM

Team principal:	Sir Frank Williams
Director of engineering:	Patrick Head
Technical director:	Sam Michael
Chief designer:	Gavin Fisher
Team manager:	Dickie Stanford
Test driver:	Nick Heidfeld
Chassis:	Williams FW27
Engine:	BMW V10
Tyres:	Michelin

Sam Michael, Williams technical director, has a tough job on his hands

MARK WEBBER

Williams loved their first tough Aussie, Alan Jones. All the signs are there that they will love Mark too, as he's a racer's racer. He's not fancy, he's totally focused, he's fully fit; there are no frills and there will be no excuses.

Mark will be raring to go when this season gets under way. For the first time in his Formula One career, he will be at the wheel of a truly competitive car. To make it even better, the first race will be on home ground in Australia, the scene of his magnificent F1 debut in 2002 when he finished an amazing fifth for Minardi.

Williams will have welcomed Mark with open arms as he's the sort of driver Sir Frank Williams and Patrick Head like, namely a straight-talking and focused competitor who'll deliver if the car is good enough. That technical director Sam Michael is a fellow Australian can only help. By the time the cars come to the grid in Australia, Mark will have enjoyed more testing than he's ever been allowed in his past three seasons with Minardi and then Jaguar. Hopefully, he will also be revelling in the horsepower that is pushed out by the BMW engine. If there is a single doubt about Mark's signing for Williams it's that, amazingly, he has never won a grand prix, which sets him apart from all other drivers signed over the years to lead this much-garlanded team. In fact, that fifth place in Melbourne three years ago remains his best result, with his best finish for Jaguar last year being sixth place at Hockenheim. However, the fact he qualified his Jaguar second at the Malaysian GP showed his true ability.

What Mark will also enjoy this year is having a team-mate with sufficient experience to help with the testing and development of the car, something that was lacking last year as Christian Klien spent time in their limited testing programme simply finding his feet. Combine this with the years of engineering experience with which Williams is blessed and you can be sure that he'll be licking his lips in anticipation.

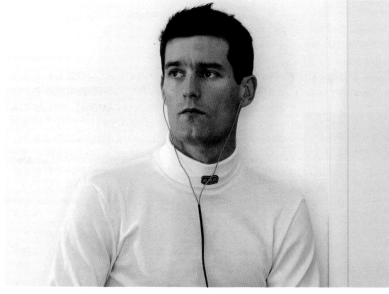

This will be Mark's biggest year by far as he's finally let loose in a competitive F1 car for the first time

TURNING POINT

There have been wins galore since Mark started racing, in everything from Formula Three to sports cars to Formula 3000, but perhaps the turning point was a victory back in 1996 when he was racing in Formula Ford. Many think they're good but soon find out they're not good enough. Not Mark. Having come to Britain in 1996 he ended up second overall at his first attempt, learning the circuits as he went. For the one-off Formula Festival at Brands Hatch at the end of the year, he wanted to put one over on team-mate and champion Kristian Kolby. And he certainly did: having passed fast-starting Jacky van der Ende in the final to win, with Kolby crashing out. This opened the way to a bigger budget from his sponsors and helped him advance to F3.

TRACK NOTES

Nationality:	AUSTRALIAN
Born:	27 AUGUST, 1976, QUEANBEYAN, AUSTRALIA
Website:	www.markwebber.com
Teams:	MINARDI 2002, JAGUAR 2003–2004, WILLIAMS 2005
First Grand Prix:	2002 AUSTRALIAN GP
Grand Prix starts:	50
Grand Prix wins:	0
	best result: fifth, 2002 Australian GP
Poles:	0
Fastest laps:	0
Points:	26
Honours:	2001 FORMULA 3000 RUNNER-UP, 1998 FIA GT RUNNER-UP, 1996 BRITISH FORMULA FORD RUNNER-UP & FORMULA FORD FESTIVAL WINNER

ANTONIO PIZZONIA

Antonio had been cast aside, but an injury to Ralf Schumacher last summer showed why Williams had kept faith with their former test driver. Then, with lawyers keeping Jenson Button in the team at BAR, he's back.

It may have taken a shoot-out with Heidfeld but Antonio is back in the saddle for 2005

TRACK NOTES

Nationality:	**BRAZILIAN**
Born:	**11 SEPTEMBER 1980, MANAUS, BRAZIL**
Website:	**www.antoniopizzonia.net**
Teams:	**JAGUAR 2003, WILLIAMS 2005**
First Grand Prix:	**2003 AUSTRALIAN GP**
Grand Prix starts:	**15**
Grand Prix wins:	**0**
Poles:	**0**
Fastest laps:	**0**
Points:	**6**

Honours: **2000 BRITISH FORMULA THREE CHAMPION, 1999 BRITISH FORMULA RENAULT CHAMPION, 1998 BRITISH FORMULA RENAULT WINTER SERIES CHAMPION, 1998 BRITISH FORMULA VAUXHALL JUNIOR CHAMPION, 1997 BRITISH FORMULA VAUXHALL JUNIOR WINTER SERIES CHAMPION, 1996 BRAZILIAN KART CHAMPION, 1992, 1993 AND 1994 PAULISTA JUNIOR KART CHAMPION, AMAZONIAN CADET KART CHAMPION**

Antonio has a lot for which to thank a trio of lawyers. After all, it was their judgement on the panel of the Contract Recognition Board that meant that Jenson Button would be staying at BAR for 2005, thus leaving a seat free for him at Williams once he'd resisted Nick Heidfeld's bid in a series of close-season shoot-outs.

Having Mark Webber as his team-mate won't be anything new for Antonio, but he won't want to be reminded of what happened the last time they were paired together, at Jaguar Racing in 2003. Mark came out of the season smelling of roses; Antonio was dropped before the year was out... Fortunately, the Brazilian has many friends at Williams, those who respected his form in testing in 2002 and it was this, as much as his three seventh-place finishes in his four outings as stand-in for the injured Ralf Schumacher last year, that earned him the nod for the team's second seat once it was clear that Button was to stay put at BAR for 2005.

"Jungle Boy" showed impressive maturity when he stood in for Schumacher. The best of his quartet of drives came in the Belgian GP, ironically the one in which he failed to finish, as he was heading for third place before he had to pull out with gearbox failure. Some might point out that Schumacher claimed a second and a fifth out of his two finishes once he returned, thus diminishing Antonio's performances.

Whether Antonio is able to become a winner remains to be seen, but he should have learned from the ups and downs of the past few years and ought to be a more focused driver as a result of this.

(**All details correct at time of going to press**)

TURNING POINT

Glance at Antonio's record before he reached Formula One and you will see that there were no turning points in the early stages of his career, just success after success for the 1996 Brazilian Karting Champion. Racing in Britain from 1997, titles were gathered every year up until he claimed the Formula Three crown. However, Formula 3000 proved a harder nut to crack. Fortunately, he found his form in the second half of the season and hit the top note at Hockenheim, fighting his way forward from sixth on the grid to second by the end of the first lap and then past Justin Wilson to take a lead he was never to lose. This show of speed helped friend Jonathan Williams to convince his father to give Antonio a deal to test for Williams, something that was to give him his Formula One salvation as a race stand-in for 2004.

McLAREN

Last year was another one to forget for McLaren as their expected bounce back to form didn't materialize.

Matters improved with the arrival of the MP4-19B, but they're going to have to do a lot better this time around.

McLaren's 2004 season improved with the MP4-19B. In 2005, Kimi Raikkonen will aim to take up where he left off

Raikkonen. Anyone who saw the pleasure that he got from edging out the Finn in last year's season-closer in Brazil will appreciate that this will be a battle worth watching, whether it's played out at the head of the field or in the pack. Rest assured, though, McLaren isn't a team that "does a Ferrari", namely ordering one of its drivers to play second fiddle to the other. That's why so many people look back more fondly to the team's period of dominance in the late 1980s – when Ayrton Senna and Alain Prost were at each other's throats all year as McLaren dominated – than they do to the

Only three teams have had periods of domination in Formula One since 1980 – Ferrari, Williams and McLaren – so don't bet against the men from Woking pressing Ferrari and Williams for honours again in the season ahead. Their pedigree is too good for them to fade away and fall back into the midfield forever.

Yes, people have talked of how team supremo Ron Dennis' eye may have been taken off the ball as he masterminded the building of his team's grandiose headquarters, the McLaren Technology Centre, but if that was the case, it is no more, as Dennis is a man who said famously that he hurt if his cars weren't winning. A sentiment such as that is good for the whole team. Once you've tasted success and crave it, winning is the only result that is good enough.

Perhaps the shake-up of the rule book for 2005 is the impetus that the team needs to prove their design and engineering excellence once again with the MP4-20 after a couple of seasons of embarrassing underachievement.

Adrian Newey will be facing his most important season for a long time and he and henchmen Neil Oatley and Mike Coughlan will have to marshall their forces very effectively to put them back on the top rung.

Continuity is something that McLaren has long practised but, for 2005, there's a major change. This comes in the driving department, with David Coulthard being dropped after nine years to be replaced by Colombian firecracker Juan Pablo Montoya, a driver who is sure to force the best out of Kimi

THE VIPS

RON DENNIS
There is no better example of a man with a dream than Ron. He started his working life as a mechanic, but soon moved into management, largely in Formula Two. His own Project Four team took control of the ailing McLaren Formula One team in 1980 and championship titles started flowing thanks to Niki Lauda, Alain Prost and then Ayrton Senna. His ambition has also led to the construction of the outstanding McLaren Technology Centre outside Woking, which also produces ultra-high-performance sports cars for Mercedes.

MARTIN WHITMARSH
Like many of the McLaren staff, Martin comes from the aerospace industry, having been manufacturing director at BAE Systems after specializing in structural analysis. He joined McLaren in 1989, initially as Head of Operations, but has subsequently been given increasing responsibility in developing the core of the McLaren group. His promotion to general manager last year means that he is now also in charge of the team's Mercedes engine operation.

way Ferrari has demanded in recent years that Michael Schumacher's passage to glory isn't blocked by Rubens Barrichello.

Engine partner and team shareholder Mercedes will have to raise its game, but the signs were there late last year that progress was being made in the horsepower department, with engine builder Ilmor eking another 20bhp out of its previously unreliable Mercedes V10. Managing director Martin Whitmarsh took responsibility for Ilmor last spring, so expect progress "under the bonnet". His position has been filled from within by Jonathan Neale. The rejigging of the technical rules means that the German manufacturer will have to make not only an even better engine, but also one that lasts for two grand prix meetings rather than one.

If Mercedes comes up trumps, Newey and his team will be really delighted. In truth, they're all desperate to cover their tracks after the nightmare of 2004, a season in which they were supposed to fight back after a poor 2003 and, largely, didn't. However, as a team of former winners with a healthy budget and a reinvigorated will to win, they are always more likely to start collecting garlands than a team to whom winning has largely been a mystery.

McLaren had looked to the MP4-19 to be a more reliable and faster version of the MP4-18 that it replaced, the car that never raced. Disappointingly, pre-season testing gave lie to the fact that it wasn't as good as they had hoped it to be. No wins followed. The MP4-19B, which was introduced mid-season

at the French GP, offered a more stable rear end under braking than the MP4-19 and, as a result, it did not eat its rear tyres as much.

Raikkonen took pole position on its second outing at the British GP. Rear-wing failure in Germany pitched the Finn out of a good position, but victory at Spa-Francorchamps two races later put the smile back on his face. Dennis was so delighted, that rumours that he might retire at the end of 2006 looked to be the furthest

thing from his mind. A third place in the Chinese GP and then being narrowly edged out of victory in the final round in Brazil augurs well for the season ahead.

Having ranked only fifth last year, McLaren is entitled to man a third car on Fridays at grand prix meetings. As erstwhile lead test driver, Pedro de la Rosa is tipped to fill this role though he was too tall to fit into the first MP4-20 chassis. This extra track time will certainly be a huge help in setting up the car.

FOR THE RECORD

Country of origin:	England
Team base:	Woking, England
Telephone:	(44) 01483 728211
Website:	www.mclaren.com
Active in Formula One:	From 1966
Grands Prix contested:	577
Wins:	138
Pole positions:	115
Fastest laps:	114

2004 DRIVERS + RESULTS

Driver	Nationality	Races	Wins	Pts	Pos
David Coulthard	British	18	-	24	10th
Kimi Raikkonen	Finnish	18	1	45	7th

THE TEAM

Team principal:	Ron Dennis
General manager:	Martin Whitmarsh
Technical director:	Adrian Newey
Director of engineering:	Neil Oatley
Chief designer:	Mike Coughlan
Chief engineer:	Steve Hallam
Team manager:	Dave Ryan
Test driver:	Alex Wurz
Engine:	Mercedes V10
Tyres:	Michelin

The Power of Dreams: Ron Dennis watches practice for the Hungarian GP, 2004

KIMI RAIKKONEN

Last season came as a shock to Kimi after he had pushed Michael Schumacher so hard in 2003. The signs are there, however, that both he and McLaren are set to come back even stronger as a result of these hard times.

Kimi appears unflappable, which is why he likes his moniker of "The Iceman". Ron Dennis likes it too, as he loves the thought of a driver akin to an ice-cold assassin at the wheel of his car, a driver who is mentally as tough as they come. So, with Juan Pablo Montoya joining him for 2005, there'll be a real case of chalk and cheese in the McLaren garage or, perhaps closer to the truth, of fire and ice...

Because he is so self-contained, Kimi isn't a driver who triggers affection from fans or even from those working in the sport. He'd rather be closeted in his room in the McLaren Communications Centre than strolling the paddock. However, everyone had to feel sorry for him in the first half of last season as he followed failure with failure. Indeed, it took the 2003 championship runner-up until the fourth round before he even finished a race. When he did, it was only in eighth. So, as you can imagine, he was hoping for reliability as well as speed from the MP4-19B when it was introduced. Pole and second place on his second outing with the car, at the British GP, showed that his prayers were being answered. Winning the Belgian GP even brought a flicker of a smile to his face, then the iceman persona slipped back into place.

One thing for sure is that Kimi will have enjoyed his mighty battle with Montoya in last year's season-closer, with the Ferraris far behind. But he won't have enjoyed the fact he got beaten, albeit only by a second, by the driver who'll be his team-mate this year: Montoya.

Over the winter, Kimi did something unusual for a driver still racing: he set up his own team. This is to run a couple of drivers in the British F3 series and has been set up with long-time manager Steve Robertson - a race winner himself in this championship in the early 1990s.

Kimi Raikkonen will have to be at his most focused to have a realistic shot at the title in 2005

TURNING POINT

After a stellar career in karting, it's safe to say that Kimi's passage through the junior car racing formulae was so rapid he hardly had time to have a turning point. Perhaps it was his management's decision to haul him out of the 1999 British Formula Renault Championship after just four races - his car wasn't competitive against Antonio Pizzonia's dominant Manor Motorsport entry - and enter him instead with Manor in the Formula Renault winter series. He went on to win four from four in that before blitzing the British series with Manor in 2000. However, it was manager Stephen Robertson's suggestion that Peter Sauber should test this driver who had yet to even try a F3 car. Whatever, Kimi impressed the F1 team boss so much that he was on the starting grid at Melbourne the following March and stunned everyone by finishing sixth.

TRACK NOTES

Nationality:	**FINNISH**
Born:	**17 OCTOBER, 1979, ESPOO, FINLAND**
Website:	**www.kimiraikkonen.com**
Teams:	**SAUBER 2001, McLAREN 2002-2005**
First Grand Prix:	**2001 AUSTRALIAN GP**
Grand Prix starts:	**68**
Grand Prix wins:	**2**
	2003 Malaysian GP, **2004** Belgian GP
Poles:	**3**
Fastest laps:	**6**
Points:	**169**
Honours:	**2003 FORMULA ONE RUNNER-UP, 2000 BRITISH FORMULA RENAULT CHAMPION, 1999 BRITISH FORMULA RENAULT WINTER SERIES CHAMPION, 1998 EUROPEAN SUPER A KART RUNNER-UP & FINNISH KART CHAMPION & NORDIC KART CHAMPION**

JUAN PABLO MONTOYA

It's all change for Juan Pablo as he moves from Williams to McLaren. How it will suit him and how he'll fare against Kimi Raikkonen will be fascinating, but the change should give the Colombian a new lease of life.

Juan Pablo Montoya has a whole new working environment for 2005. Whether he thrives remains to be seen

petulant, manner may be forgiven. Indeed, the fighting characteristics he showed in winning last year's final round in Brazil will have excited Dennis no end, particularly the way he battled side-by-side down the pitlane with Raikkonen and then jumped him on the exit.

Juan Pablo will also be out for wins as 2004 produced just two podium visits before that final round, a thin diet for a driver who was once tipped as Michael Schumacher's heir apparent. This year, he'll want to prove he's still the man to topple Schumacher, but you can be sure that his team-mate will be out to prove otherwise. To understand how Juan Pablo intends to take battle to the Finn, check out his new helmet design: a block of ice being warmed with a blowtorch...

Four years with Williams have made Juan Pablo the driver he is. So it will be interesting to see how he adapts to the McLaren way of doing things. It's a sure-fire bet that the first change will be a physical one as McLaren supremo Ron Dennis said before the end of last season that he was sure his team would get more from Juan Pablo both mentally and physically. Indeed, one glance at the porky Colombian celebrating his win in last year's season-closer showed they have plenty of material with which to work...

As for the mental side of things, Ron can famously nurture his drivers to give of their best if he feels that something is preventing them from achieving their potential. How Juan Pablo slips into the role of being an ambassador for McLaren as he's put onto the merry-go-round of sponsor functions remains to be seen. It may emphasize just what a gem McLaren had in the gentlemanly and erudite David Coulthard.

However, as long as Juan Pablo delivers on the track, his sometimes brusque, and even

TRACK NOTES

Nationality:	COLOMBIAN
Born:	20 SEPTEMBER, 1975, BOGOTA, COLOMBIA
Website:	www.jpmontoya.com
Teams:	WILLIAMS 2001–2004, McLAREN 2005
First Grand Prix:	2001 AUSTRALIAN GP
Grand Prix starts:	68
Grand Prix wins:	4
2001 Italian GP, 2003 Monaco GP, German GP, 2004 Brazilian GP	
Poles:	11
Fastest laps:	11
Points:	221
Honours: 2000 INDY 500 WINNER, 1999 INDYCAR CHAMPION, 1998 FORMULA 3000 CHAMPION	

TURNING POINT

There has never been any doubt Juan Pablo possesses extraordinary raw speed and it was shown most clearly when he burst onto the Formula 3000 scene in 1997 after a patchy two-year spell in F3. The extra power suited him perfectly and his domination of the second round on the tricky street circuit at Pau had his rivals gasping as he qualified on pole and won by 35s from Tom Kristensen, who would go on to win Le Mans six times and lapped many who fancied themselves. Too many mistakes followed, though, and Ricardo Zonta ended the year as champion, with Juan Pablo two points behind. He made amends in 1998, pipping Nick Heidfeld to the crown, but found no ride in F1 so headed Stateside and became the Champ Car champion in 1999 and an Indy 500 winner in 2000 before making it to F1 in 2001.

SAUBER

In Jacques Villeneuve, perennial midfield runners Sauber are fielding a world champion for the first time.

Whether he can propel the Swiss team to success, or even whether he can beat Felipe Massa, remains to be seen.

Felipe Massa will want to show he is the team's top driver ahead of incoming ex-World Champion Jacques Villeneuve in Sauber's final year with Ferrari engines

There are only two Formula One world champions on the grid this year: Michael Schumacher and Jacques Villeneuve. So, the fact that little Sauber has one of them at the wheel of one of its cars is quite an achievement. In fact, the deal came together as a major surprise to everyone in the sport. After all, Villeneuve had spent a year on the sidelines. Unlike Schumacher, though, the 1997 world champion is unlikely to have a winning car beneath him and he will have to cast his mind back to his title-winning season for the last of his 11 wins.

Villeneuve will also have to contend with a firebrand of a team-mate in Felipe Massa. In fact, he might get on well with the hard-charging Brazilian, who led last year's Brazilian GP fleetingly, although Jacques famously does not make friends with team-mates, preferring instead to have the team built around himself. This time, though, Massa is the one who is established with the team and Villeneuve the incomer. How this develops will be worth watching.

A sixth-place ranking in the constructors' championship last year was a repeat of Sauber's 2003 mark, one below its 2002 standing which, in turn, had been a place down on its best-ever season in 2001 when they ranked fourth. Looking at the ingredients for the season ahead, even with the curve-ball of new technical regulations that include slashing downforce, it's hard to see the Swiss team making up any lost ground.

THE VIPS

PETER SAUBER

Here's a man who is the complete opposite of Renault's showman Flavio Briatore. In fact, he's all but invisible, but that's just how this taciturn Swiss likes it. A builder of sportscars in the 1970s, he made his breakthrough by fitting a Mercedes engine to his 1984 chassis, starting a relationship that led to him running the German marque's sportscar department and winning the Sportscar World Championship and the Le Mans 24 Hours in 1989 before forming his own F1 team for 1993.

SEAMUS MULLARKEY

Sauber's head of aerodynamics started out in F1 with March in 1990. A move to Fomet in 1991 lasted for a year before Seamus moved on to Larrousse where he added data acquisition to his job role of aerodynamicist. Moving away from F1 in 1995, he worked at GenTec and then Galmer Engineering, designing software, before making his F1 comeback with Jordan in 1996. His move to Sauber came in 1998 and he has worked under the guidance of technical director Willy Rampf ever since.

Think of Sauber and it really is like a Swiss watch: solid and dependable, but not flash. The description also fits team principal Peter Sauber, a man who is the very opposite of Renault's flamboyant Flavio Briatore. He is a man of mettle, though, as shown at last year's final race when he went against the advice of Ferrari's Jean Todt by putting his name to an agreement signed by all the other team principals for a package of cost-cutting rule changes for this season. All the principals except Todt, that is. Don't forget that this took bravery, as it is from Ferrari, of course, that Sauber gets its engines and Ferrari sees Sauber as its pawn in negotiations as a result.

The closeness of that relationship could be seen when Sauber was hit with pre-season jibes last year that its C23 was a straight copy of the previous year's Ferrari, the F2003-GA, but perhaps this wasn't surprising as not only was Sauber using a Ferrari engine (badged as a Petronas again), but

also a Ferrari gearbox. If you look at it this way, the shape made sense. It was worth noting, too, that the team was not one year behind Ferrari on engine spec as it had been in the years since it signed the deal to run Ferrari engines, but that it was running the same V10s following the introduction of the one-engine-per-meeting rule that meant that a new specification of engine was required. More of a surprise, though, came last spring when Sauber ditched the twin-keel design that it had championed for three years – it was probably for this reason that the Swiss outfit turned to Ferrari because they needed some guidance on what was best for a single-keel car.

Not surprisingly for such a conservative team, the C23 contained no bold innovations. Perhaps those are being saved for its successor, this year's C24, which will be the first car designed in full conjunction with the team's new wind tunnel. If so, expect a step forward. It may even afford the team's

drivers the luxury of not having to resort to crafty pitstop strategies to find their way ahead of the drivers in front of them in races, something that both Giancarlo Fisichella – who Sauber sportingly allowed to move on to Renault for 2005 to further his chances – and Massa did with aplomb last year.

There is another factor that may alter the lie of the land for Sauber. The team has swapped tyre suppliers from Bridgestone to Michelin, with Peter Sauber saying that it would help against the

other similarly shod teams in the midfield.

One thing that will remain constant is the difference between Sauber's budget and those of the teams ahead of them. This was made apparent by the comparative lack of testing undertaken by Fisichella and Massa. It was also shown by the fact that, although Sauber was entitled to run a third driver in the practice sessions on the Fridays of grand prix meetings last year, it elected not to do so, thus losing valuable set-up findings.

FOR THE RECORD

Country of origin:	**Switzerland**
Team base:	**Hinwil, Switzerland**
Telephone:	**(41) 1937 9000**
Website:	**www.sauber-petronas.com**
Active in Formula One:	**From 1993**
Grands Prix contested:	**198**
Wins:	**0**
Pole positions:	**0**
Fastest laps:	**0**

2004 DRIVERS + RESULTS

Driver	Nationality	Races	Wins	Pts	Pos
Giancarlo Fisichella	**Italian**	18	–	22	11th
Felipe Massa	**Brazilian**	18	–	12	12th

THE TEAM

Team principal:	**Peter Sauber**
Technical director:	**Willy Rampf**
Engine director:	**Osamu Goto**
Chief designer:	**Seamus Mullarkey**
Chief engineer:	**Jacky Eeckelaert**
Team manager:	**Beat Zehnder**
Test/Third driver:	**tba**
Chassis:	**Sauber C24**
Engine:	**Petronas Ferrari V10**
Tyres:	**Michelin**

Peter Sauber had the guts last year to stand up to engine-supplier Ferrari

FELIPE MASSA

Last year provided clear proof that, in terms of technique, Felipe had grown from boy to man and that the rough edges in his driving had been smoothed out. Now he's out to pit his skills against Jacques Villeneuve.

The maturing process of Felipe was one of the major focal points last season for those who watch F1 in depth. Indeed, the form of the Sauber drivers isn't always obvious as they go about their business quietly in the midfield, but Felipe wasn't humbled by the presence of an acknowledged highly ranked driver, Giancarlo Fisichella, ending up 12-6 down on qualifying and proving that the time he spent testing for Ferrari in 2003 had helped take the rough edges

off his driving style. This season Felipe will have another yardstick by which to measure his progress: 1997 world champion Jacques Villeneuve. Some will say that, on the evidence of his weak form on his return for the final three races of last season, Jacques is past it, but the French Canadian will be back to his best this time around and, for once, he will not be featuring in a team that has been built around his every whim.

The cheery Brazilian is actually fortunate to be racing this season, fortunate even to be still alive, as he endured a 113g impact when he shunted in last year's Canadian GP and the FIA president, Max Mosley, is one of many who feel that his life was saved by the mandatory HANS head and shoulder brace.

Felipe will be looking to build upon the series of strong performances that he recorded last year, such as his fifth place at Monaco, his career-best fourth place in the Belgian GP and leading a couple of laps in his home race in Brazil. To this end, he will be hoping that the first Sauber produced entirely in the team's wind tunnel will have the aerodynamic advances that the team has always lacked.

Felipe Massa gives the thumbs-up but will he have anything to celebrate in the season ahead?

TURNING POINT

Making the right move, choosing the right formula or even the right team can make or break a career and, after showing strong form to win the Brazilian Formula Chevrolet at his second attempt in 1999 and then the European Formula Renault title in 2000, Felipe broke with tradition. Instead of moving up to F3, he moved up to Formula 3000, albeit to the second division Euro F3000 series. So, to prove that this was the right move, he had to start winning. And win he did, right from the opening round. This was at Vallelunga. Racing for the Draco team, he slotted his car on pole and was never headed, giving him plenty to celebrate on his 20th birthday three days later. That he went on to clinch the title and attract the attention of Sauber, who helped him into F1 in 2002, proved his choice had been the right one.

TRACK NOTES

Nationality:	**BRAZILIAN**
Born:	**25 APRIL, 1981, SAO PAULO, BRAZIL**
Website:	**www.felipemassa.com**
Teams:	**SAUBER 2002 & 2004-2005**
First Grand Prix:	**2002 AUSTRALIAN GP**
Grand Prix starts:	**34**
Grand Prix wins:	**0**
	best result: fourth, **2004** Belgian GP
Poles:	**0**
Fastest laps:	**0**
Points:	**16**
Honours:	**2001 EUROPEAN FORMULA 3000 CHAMPION, 2000 EUROPEAN & ITALIAN FORMULA RENAULT CHAMPION, 1999 BRAZILIAN FORMULA CHEVROLET CHAMPION**

JACQUES VILLENEUVE

F1 needs drivers with something to say. So it's good to welcome Jacques back. However, on the track, we'll be looking for Jacques the driver of old, not the Jacques who struggled with Renault at the end of last year.

Back in the big time once more, Jacques Villeneuve poses alongside Sauber team principal Peter Sauber

It seems a long time ago since Jacques and Michael Schumacher were slugging it out in the final round of the 1997 world championship. Indeed, as he struggled to make an impression with BAR, a whole generation of fans has grown up in the interim, unaware he was a driver who used to put the wind up the mighty German.

It's said that you never forget how to ride a bike, so, in that vein, Jacques ought to be able to crank himself up to his optimum operating level with Sauber by the time the campaign kicks off in Australia in March. If he wants to prove to Peter Sauber that he is capable of being the calibre of driver that the Swiss team boss hopes he has signed, Jacques will have to raise his game to a higher level than that shown when he replaced Jarno Trulli at Renault for the final three grands prix of last season. He finished each of them, but never higher than tenth. There were mitigating circumstances, in that he hardly had any testing time in the car before those three flyaways. Many, though, thought the problem lay with his fitness after 11 months away from racing. If that's all it was, rather than a loss of talent, then Jacques will simply have to work extra hard over the winter.

One thing for sure is that Jacques will find the atmosphere at Sauber very different to the one at BAR which became so politically charged as the various factions fought and Jacques himself was found surplus to requirements for 2004. He'll also be delighted Sauber has a very low PR profile, which will keep him free from those sponsor functions that he loathes so much.

TRACK NOTES

Nationality:	CANADIAN
Born:	9 APRIL 1971, ST JEAN-SUR-RICHELIEU, CANADA
Website:	www.jacques.villeneuve.com
Teams:	WILLIAMS 1996–98, BAR 1999–2003; RENAULT 2004; SAUBER 2005
First Grand Prix:	1996 AUSTRALIAN GP
Grand Prix starts:	136
Grand Prix wins:	11
	1996 European GP, British GP, Hungarian GP, Portuguese GP **1997** Brazilian GP, Argentinian GP, Spanish GP, British GP, Hungarian GP, Austrian GP, Luxembourg GP
Poles:	13
Fastest laps:	9
Points:	213
Honours:	1997 FORMULA ONE CHAMPION, 1996 FORMULA ONE RUNNER-UP, 1995 INDYCAR CHAMPION AND INDY 500 WINNER, 1994 INDYCAR ROOKIE OF THE YEAR, 1993 TOYOTA ATLANTIC ROOKIE OF THE YEAR, 1992 JAPANESE FORMULA THREE RUNNER-UP

TURNING POINT

The Monaco GP, the Le Mans 24 Hours and the Indy 500 are seen as motor racing's triple crown. So it's not surprising that winning the Indy 500 really launched Jacques' career. With a father as well-known as the flamboyant Gilles, Jacques was always going to suffer in comparison, but his form improved during a three-year spell in Italian F3. Moving to Japanese F3 in 1992 made him look better still, as did a move to the North American Toyota Atlantic series, but it was his graduation to Indycar racing that really did the trick. A win came in his first season, but it was victory in the 1995 Indy 500, ahead of Christian Fittipaldi, that convinced Bernie Ecclestone it was time that F1 fans had the Villeneuve name back, encouraging Williams to find a ride for him for 1996. Jacques bagged the title the following year for good measure.

RED BULL RACING

It was only at the 11th hour that the Jaguar Racing of old was saved, with Red Bull drinks company owner Dietrich Mateschitz buying the team from Ford last November and agreeing to keep on the staff for the season ahead.

From the back seat to the driver's position, can Red Bull give Jaguar wings?

Only a flurry of deals in the rush to the mid-November deadline for registering for the 2005 World Championship led to what was once Jaguar Racing being saved so that it could emerge for this year's action as Red Bull Racing, meaning that 10 teams will be going out to battle after all. There had been interest aplenty in buying the team, but three other suitors were rejected for failing to meet the criteria applied by the vendors. These included having the funds to keep the team running for three years in order to guarantee the jobs of Jaguar Racing's 350 employees, thus meeting American employment law. Jaguar Racing's parent company was American motor manufacturer Ford.

Dietrich Mateschitz, the Austrian billionaire owner of the Red Bull energy drinks brand, was the man who pulled off the deal, achieving his long-held dream of owning a team after being a major backer of Sauber. One of the sticking points was that he didn't want to buy engine-builder Cosworth as well. However, had Ford tarried too long in pressing him to, they would have missed the deadline, leaving the team with no value. In the end, Cosworth was bought by Champ Car team owners Kevin Kalkhoven and Gerald Forsythe, with the agreement that they would continue to build a V10, this to be used both by Red Bull Racing and Minardi.

So, with the deal done, allegedly for $1, the personnel who'd worked so hard in Jaguar Racing's final year kept their jobs, though principal Tony Purnell and MD David Pitchforth were later replaced by Christian Horner and former tech boss Gunther Steiner. These were the people who had helped Mark Webber and Christian Klien to guide the team to seventh overall in the constructors' championship, finishing a point ahead of Toyota. While this wasn't enough to make the team worry Renault, Sauber or BAR, it was an impressive achievement given that their budget was only $130m compared to Toyota's $400m. The highlight on the track was Webber qualifying second for the Malaysian GP, although race results never got close to this, with sixth place their best showing.

FOR THE RECORD

Country of origin:	**England**
Team base:	**Milton Keynes, England**
Telephone:	**(44) 01908 279700**
Website:	**www.redbull.com**
Active in Formula One:	**From 1997 (as Stewart until 2000)**
Grands Prix contested:	**134**
Wins:	**1**
Pole positions:	**1**
Fastest laps:	**0**

2004 DRIVERS + RESULTS

Driver	Nationality	Races	Wins	Pts	Pos
Christian Klien	**Austrian**	18	-	3	16th
Mark Webber	**Australian**	18	-	7	13th

THE TEAM

Sporting director:	**Christian Horner**
Technical director:	**Gunther Steiner**
Director of engineering:	**Ian Pocock**
Chief aerodynamicist:	**Ben Agathangelou**
Chief designer:	**Rob Taylor**
Chief engineer:	**tba**
Third driver:	**Vitantonio Liuzzi**
Chassis:	**Red Bull R5b**
Engine:	**Cosworth V10**
Tyres:	**Michelin**

DAVID COULTHARD

After 11 years, David Coulthard was out of Formula One. But then

he signed a one-year contract to lead the new Red Bull Racing team.

Eclipsed by Kimi Raikkonen over the past two seasons, David's days at McLaren were numbered. Indeed, he knew even before the start of the 2004 campaign that he was to be replaced by Juan Pablo Montoya for 2005. It looked as though Jaguar Racing would take up his services. But then the team folded and it was only after lengthy consideration that Dietrich Mateschitz came round to the idea that he needed an established grand prix winner to lead his squad rather than two young hotshots. And thus David secured his Formula One future, for this year at least.

The deal is reported to be worth more than $2 million, with a bonus of $100,000 for every point scored. Unless the team makes progress, this might not amount to a whole lot more, but David will be expected to pick up occasional scraps from the top table by using his experience as well as his speed. He will be out, too, to restore his reputation which suffered last year when his best finish was fourth in the German Grand Prix. There were mistakes, too, but the 33-year-old Scot will be anxious to put those behind him and try his best to remind people of why he has 13 grand prix wins to his name, fewer only than the dominant Michael Schumacher among today's ranks of Formula One drivers.

TRACK NOTES

Nationality:	**SCOTTISH**
Born:	**27 MARCH, 1971, TWYNHOLM, SCOTLAND**
Website:	**www.davidcoulthard-f1.com**
Teams:	**WILLIAMS 1994-1995, McLAREN 1996-2004, RED BULL 2005**
First Grand Prix:	**1994 SPANISH GP**
Grand Prix starts:	**175**
Grand Prix wins:	**13**
	1995 Portuguese GP, **1997** Australian GP, Italian GP, **1998** San Marino GP, **1999** British GP, Belgian GP, **2000** British GP, Monaco GP, French GP, **2001** Brazilian GP, Austrian GP, **2002** Monaco GP, **2003** Australian GP
Poles:	**12**
Fastest laps:	**18**
Points:	**475**
Honours:	**2001 FORMULA ONE RUNNER-UP**

CHRISTIAN KLIEN

Christian was helped into Formula One with Jaguar last year by sponsor

Red Bull and keeps his place largely thanks to Red Bull buying the team.

Christian kept his ride after a shoot-out with Vitantonio Liuzzi who is waiting in the wings to take over if Christian struggles this year. He was something of an unknown when he broke into F1 with Jaguar last year, arriving as winner of the Marlboro Masters Formula Three invitation race at Zandvoort and runner-up in the European F3 Championship. If truth be told, he was still something of an unknown by the end of it. Save, of course, for proving something of a magnet for David Coulthard in the late-season races, thus guaranteeing television coverage as they clashed, most notably at Spa-Francorchamps.

The key to Christian's ascent up the racing ladder is backing from Red Bull and, just as it looked as though his season at the sport's top table was to prove his only one and he was starting to look for a test ride with another team so that he could stay in F1, his mentor Dietrich Mateschitz bought the crumbling Jaguar Racing.

The only point of comparison for Christian's maiden season in Formula One is Mark Webber. With points hard to come by, Webber collected but seven points all year, making Christian's tally of three look not too shoddy. However, Christian wasn't rated by his team-mate and was outqualified by him on 15 of the 18 grands prix though it's fair to say the team was very much built around the Australian.

(All details correct at time of going to press)

TRACK NOTES

Nationality:	**AUSTRIAN**
Born:	**7 FEBRUARY, 1983, HOHENEMS, AUSTRIA**
Website:	**www.christian-klien.com**
Teams:	**JAGUAR 2004, RED BULL RACING 2005**
First Grand Prix:	**2004 AUSTRALIAN GP**
Grand Prix starts:	**18**
Grand Prix wins:	**0**
	best result: sixth, **2004** Belgian GP
Poles:	**0**
Fastest laps:	**0**
Points:	**3**
Honours:	**2003 EUROPEAN FORMULA THREE RUNNER-UP, 2003 MARLBORO MASTERS WINNER, 2002 GERMAN FORMULA RENAULT CHAMPION, 1996 SWISS KADET KART CHAMPION**

TOYOTA

Toyota has now clocked up three seasons in Formula One, but are still to record a win or, for that matter, any visits to the podium. This year will be the one when they really must make progress commensurate with their lavish budget. Those in the know predict success in the future, but this could well be a long time in coming.

Spray and go: Jarno Trulli in practice for last year's Japanese Grand Prix

On the form of its first three years in Formula One, it would be easy to write Toyota off as a team that's never going to achieve anything. But that would be to ignore the undercurrent of what has been happening through 2004. Sure, only nine points were scored, fully seven less than in their second year, but all the progress made was made behind the scenes.

First off, Toyota has recruited by far its strongest driver line-up yet, in grand prix winners Ralf Schumacher and Jarno Trulli.

Secondly, the TF105 will be the first chassis that has been the true work of technical director Mike Gascoyne. Judging by the successes he achieved at Tyrrell, Jordan and Renault, the Englishman ought to come up trumps and produce a chassis that will make the most of the ample horsepower that has been one of the team's few strong points since they made their debut in Formula One in 2002.

Thirdly, the team is considering a swap to Bridgestone tyres for 2006 and beyond. This could be an inspired decision judging by the way that Bridgestone rose to the challenge in 2004 and produced some tyres that performed really well in hot conditions, something that had previously been their Achilles' heel. Such a change shows the team is looking ahead.

If Toyota is to advance from being at the back of the midfield bunch and thus only an occasional forager of points as the top teams stumble, then it must draw on the experience it has gained and temper it with the knowledge of its personnel from their time with other teams. Looking at the huge budget that Toyota is throwing at making its Formula One team a success, all of the sport's insiders feel sure that race wins will follow. It's just a question of when this team, with a budget that outstrips even that spent by Ferrari, will hit the top.

FOR THE RECORD

Country of origin:	**Germany (Japan)**
Team base:	**Cologne, Germany**
Telephone:	**(49) 2234 18230**
Website:	**www.toyota-f1.com**
Active in Formula One:	**from 2002**
Grands Prix contested:	**51**
Wins:	**0**
Pole positions:	**0**
Fastest laps:	**0**

2004 DRIVERS + RESULTS

Driver	Nationality	Races	Wins	Pts	Pos
Cristiano da Matta	**Brazilian**	12	-	3	17th
Olivier Panis	**French**	17	-	6	14th
Jarno Trulli	**Italian**	2	-	-	N/A
Ricardo Zonta	**Brazilian**	5	-	-	N/A

THE TEAM

Team principal:	**Tsutomo Tomita**
President:	**John Howett**
Technical director:	**Mike Gascoyne**
Engine director:	**Luca Marmorini**
Chief designer:	**Gustav Brunner**
Chief engineer:	**Dieter Gass**
Team manager:	**Richard Cregan**
Third driver:	**Ricardo Zonta**
Test driver:	**Olivier Panis**
Chassis:	**Toyota TF105**
Engine:	**Toyota V10**
Tyres:	**Michelin**

RALF SCHUMACHER

Ralf won't look back fondly at his final season with Williams after he hit a wall at Indianapolis and missed six races. But now he's back with Toyota.

It will seem strange to see Ralf's helmet sticking out of the cockpit of a Toyota this season as he'd almost become part of the furniture at Williams.

No longer will he have debriefs with Patrick Head and long-time ally Sam Michael but with Mike Gascoyne instead. The English tech chief is another person with whom Ralf goes back a long way, with the two of them having worked together at Jordan back in 1998. Theirs should be a fruitful relationship, as Ralf possesses a strong ability to sort a chassis, something that was shown by Williams' upturn in form when he returned from injury at the end of last season.

Overall, missing a third of a season's grands prix is never going to help a driver's ranking, but nor is being disqualified from what was, up to then, his best race of the year, a fate which befell Ralf when he lost second place in the Canadian GP because his car's brake ducts were too large.

The season ahead will be all about rebuilding Ralf in an environment that is less prickly than at Williams. Certainly, he'll find Jarno Trulli a less in-your-face team-mate than Juan Pablo Montoya. Equally, he'll do well to spend more time with the team, crack the occasional joke and, basically, "be one of the boys". Toyota may not be known for having a laugh, but it can only help keep things in perspective.

TRACK NOTES

Nationality:	**GERMAN**
Born:	**30 JUNE, 1975, KERPEN, GERMANY**
Website:	**www.ralf-schumacher.de**
Teams:	**JORDAN 1997-1998, WILLIAMS 1999-2004, TOYOTA 2005**
First Grand Prix:	**1997 AUSTRALIAN GP**
Grand Prix starts:	**128**
Grand Prix wins:	**6**
	2001 San Marino GP, Canadian GP, German GP, **2002** Malaysian GP, **2003** European GP, French GP
Poles:	**5**
Fastest laps:	**7**
Points:	**249**
Honours:	**1996 FORMULA NIPPON CHAMPION, 1995 GERMAN FORMULA THREE RUNNER-UP & MACAU GP WINNER, 1993 GERMAN FORMEL JUNIOR RUNNER-UP**

JARNO TRULLI

Few drivers give their team its only win of the season and get dropped, but this is what happened to Jarno last year. Now the Italian is with Toyota.

It's said that Jarno is a driver who needs to feel loved if he is going to give of his best. It's also safe to say that he didn't always feel so at Renault. Indeed, there were already rumours that team principal Flavio Briatore wanted to replace him for 2005 when Jarno finally scored the first grand prix win that his talents had been suggesting since he arrived in F1 in 1997. That the win came at Monaco was all the more impressive, as he led from pole and resisted enormous pressure from BAR's Jenson Button. However, when he lost concentration four races later, allowing Rubens Barrichello to steal by for third place, the writing was on the wall; Renault's hierarchy were convinced. His season fell apart, the bond of trust snapped and his confidence was broken. Renault showed him the door early, and his seat was filled for the rest of the season by Jacques Villeneuve, giving the Italian time to have two races for Toyota.

Jarno needs a new start for 2005. Indeed, he deserves one, as he remains one of the purest driving skills in Formula One and perhaps even the best of all over a single qualifying lap. Some say he's overly analytical, not an aggressive enough racer, others that he simply needs the right environment. Reunited with Mike Gascoyne at Toyota, the Englishman having held the technical reins at Renault in 2002, Jarno will be key to taking the Japanese manufacturer where it wants to go. In fact, the move could have come at just the right time for both parties.

TRACK NOTES

Nationality:	**ITALIAN**
Born:	**13 JULY, 1974, PESCARA, ITALY**
Website:	**www.jarnotrulli.com**
Teams:	**MINARDI 1997, PROST 1997-1999, JORDAN 2000-2001, RENAULT 2002-2004, TOYOTA 2005**
First Grand Prix:	**1997 AUSTRALIAN GP**
Grand Prix starts:	**130**
Grand Prix wins:	**1**
	2004 Monaco GP
Poles:	**2**
Fastest laps:	**0**
Points:	**117**
Honours:	**1996 GERMAN FORMULA THREE CHAMPION, 1994 WORLD KART CHAMPION**

JORDAN

Jordan struggled for budget last year and spent much of the winter seeking a new owner in a battle to survive.

Golden shot: Jordan's Giorgio Pantano failed to come up trumps in 2004

No team on the F1 grid makes it clearer how hard it is to stay on the pace in Formula One if you don't have a budget to rival those of your opponents. One of just two non-manufacturer teams, Jordan's decline from title-challengers in 1999 to the team second from the back was all too clear. Sadly, a small budget inevitably means little progress. In fact, as the top teams pull away, it means regression, which isn't a word you'd readily associate with Eddie Jordan.

Through much of 2004, there was talk that he'd had enough and was looking to duck out, with rumours that the Al Maktoum family from Dubai were looking to take control. But these faded out, meaning the team HQ wouldn't have to be relocated, that EJ would stay on as figurehead and that a purchaser was still being sought as the movers and shakers from Dubai swung their attention to starting a completely new team under the wing of McLaren.

In November, talk turned to the arrival of a Chinese businessman, Guo Jie, who wanted control, albeit leaving the reins in the hands of EJ. He had a rival in former Formula 3000 team owner Christian Horner, who had gathered funds from venture capitalists that enabled him to take over the helm of the team, having paid the Irish team founder around £30m for his 50.1 per cent share.

One other confusing factor last summer was what engines the team would be using, as Ford's decision to quit F1 left the team without an engine for 2005. Then Toyota was lined up to supply customer engines for the first time, with Ford said to be contributing to the team's budget as a result of not having fulfilled its 2005 engine deal...

Part of the Toyota deal was expected to be a ride for Ryan Briscoe, a Toyota development driver since 2001, but he headed off for the Indy Racing League as he couldn't find his part of the budget.

At the time of going to press, neither a new owner nor the identity of either driver could be revealed for certain.

On the design side, there's good news in that Mark Smith rejoined Jordan from Renault last August, joining John McQuilliam, who held together the design side after Henri Durand quit last March. Nicolo Petrucci remains as the leading aerodynamicist.

FOR THE RECORD

Country of origin:	**England**
Team base:	**Silverstone, England**
Telephone:	**(44) 01327 850800**
Website:	**www.f1jordan.com**
Active in Formula One:	**From 1991**
Grands Prix contested:	**231**
Wins:	**4**
Pole positions:	**2**
Fastest laps:	**2**

2004 DRIVERS + RESULTS

Driver	Nationality	Races	Wins	Pts	Pos
Timo Glock	**German**	4	-	2	19th
Nick Heidfeld	**German**	18	-	3	18th
Giorgio Pantano	**Italian**	14	-	-	N/A

THE TEAM

Team principal:	**Eddie Jordan**
Technical director:	**James Robinson**
Chief designer:	**John McQuilliam**
Chief engineer:	**Gerry Hughes**
Team manager:	**Tim Edwards**
Third driver:	**tba**
Chassis:	**Jordan EJ15**
Engine:	**Toyota V10**
Tyres:	**Bridgestone**

ROBERT DOORNBOS

At the time of going to press, Robert Doornbos looked set to be one of Jordan's drivers. He came to racing via an unusual route, though.

Robert could have been a tennis star, but a chance visit as a guest to the Belgian GP as recently as the autumn of 1998 turned his life right around. After that, it was all racing. So, with no karting background, he leapt straight into single-seaters in 1999. And, six seasons working his way up the ladder, he's ready to race in Formula One.

Although a Formula 3000 racer last year, with the crack Arden squad, ranking as the top rookie in third overall while team-mate Vitantonio Liuzzi dominated, Robert has already got some Formula One experience under his belt as he became Jordan's third driver once Timo Glock stepped up to the team's second race seat when Giorgio Pantano was dropped for the final three races of the season.

The experience that Robert gained in the Friday sessions will have helped enormously, and he really impressed, helping in no small part to attract the backers to land him a full-time ride.

Indeed, there will be something approaching Formula One fever in his home land if he finally did land this ride, as Holland has been deprived of a representative at the sport's top level since Jos Verstappen dropped out. Now, like London buses, two come along at once, as compatriot

TRACK NOTES

Nationality:	**Dutch**
Born:	**23 September 1981, ROTTERDAM, HOLLAND**
Website:	**www.robertdoornbos.com**
Teams:	**JORDAN 2005**
First Grand Prix:	**2005 Australian GP**
Grand Prix starts:	**0**
Grand Prix wins:	**0**
Poles:	**0**
Fastest laps:	**0**
Points:	**0**
Honours:	**2000 BENELUX FORMULA FORD RUNNER-UP, 1999 BRITISH VAUXHALL LOTUS WINTER SERIES RUNNER-UP**

Christijan Albers will be racing for Minardi.
(**All details correct at time of going to press**)

JORDAN NUMBER TWO

The lack of knowledge over who would own the team hampered drivers selection at Jordan in a major way last winter, which is why the team had no clear picture of who would drive its second car as we closed for press at the start of January, with all hopeful drivers required to bring a considerable pot of money to the team.

Australian driver Ryan Briscoe had appeared to be a shoo-in for one of the Jordan rides for 2005 once the deal was signed for the team to run with Toyota engines, especially as he had been a Toyota-backed driver since 2001. However, he was unable to bring the rest of the budget and instead opted for a paid drive in the Indy Racing League with a team powered by Toyota engines, eyeing his break in Formula One with the works Toyota team in seasons to come.

Timo Glock – who raced briefly for the team last year, stepping up from the test ride to stand in for Giorgio Pantano when he was dropped after a payment dispute to score a couple of points on his debut in Canada – seemed like the driver most likely to race for the team along with Robert Doornbos and Richard Lyons. Glock was thought to have close to a hefty budget to play with from former team sponsor DHL which he might bring to the party, making his re-signing doubly attractive.

The final one of this trio is Ulsterman Lyons who enjoyed a bumper season in which he followed the likes of Pedro de la Rosa and Ralf Schumacher in winning the Formula Nippon single-seater title in Japan.

For good measure, he also won the All-Japan GT series for the works Nissan team but ran out of time when chasing the funds to make his Formula One debut for Jordan in the Japanese Grand Prix.

For a brief while in December, when Alex Shnaider's Midland outfit got into talks with Jordan as they considered bringing forward their move into Formula One by a year by buying Jordan, Mexican driver Mario Dominguez came into the frame, primed to make the move across from Champ Cars.

But then that deal fell out of bed, Christian Horner's financial takeover bid went notably quiet and Eddie Jordan looked to be back in control of selecting his drivers for 2005, not that he managed to do so before Christmas 2004 as he fought to sort the good financial deals from the duff ones. And all this when he could tempt drivers with a strong Toyota engine...

(**All details correct at time of going to press**)

MINARDI

Try as they might, winning a grand prix is never going to be on Minardi's agenda. Their greatest triumph is simply to be on the grid at all, as the cost of competing in Formula One remains so prohibitively sky high.

Knight Rider: Gianmaria Bruni failed to help Minardi to any points in 2004

Team principal Paul Stoddart might run the least successful team in Formula One today, but the feisty Australian became the saviour of the world championship at the end of last season when he led the campaign to slash costs.

Perhaps he led the fight because he was the one who would suffer the most if the costs kept spiralling, but perhaps it was simply because he likes a good scrap and stands up for his principles. Either way, Formula One fans are in his debt for the way he has stuck his neck out to try and improve the world's top racing formula.

It's safe to say that 2004 wasn't an easy season for the Anglo-Italian team, but the team did at least improve on its 2003 form by scoring a point, at the US GP, when the usually less-than-sparkling Zsolt Baumgartner showed at the US GP that his steady approach could garner results as he benefitted from a race of attrition to finish eighth. Stoddart pointed this out in no uncertain terms to his faster,

but more flighty, team-mate Gianmaria Bruni.

This single point was unlikely to be added to, but Stoddart's joy was shattered a month later when team manager John Walton died of a heart attack just before the British GP. To add insult to injury, Ford then quit Formula One, leaving the team without an engine for 2005, this despite having extended its deal with Cosworth just two weeks earlier. Annoyingly, the new rule demanding that engines must last for two grands prix would have dictated that Minardi would have had the same engine as Jaguar Racing. Luckily, Cosworth was saved and the team will enjoy the same engines as Red Bull Racing.

If the engine is going to be less competitive, the chassis is likely to be even more so, with aerodynamicist Loic Bigois having left for Williams before the first race last year with the result that this year's chassis is effectively at least two years old and very tired, to say nothing of the fact that it shows no

innovation whatsoever. Running with a budget a tenth the size of big-spending Toyota can be severely limiting. The final part of the package, the drivers, is again down to who can bring a sensible budget to the team, with Christijan Albers and whoever becomes the number two hoping this is their first port of call in a long F1 career.

FOR THE RECORD

Country of origin:	Italy
Team base:	Ledbury, England & Faenza, Italy
Telephone:	(39) 0546 696111
Website:	www.minardi.it
Active in Formula One:	From 1985
Grands Prix contested:	322
Wins:	0
Pole positions:	0
Fastest laps:	0

2004 DRIVERS + RESULTS

Driver	Nationality	Races	Wins	Pts	Pos
Gianmaria Bruni	**Italian**	18	-	-	N/A
Zsolt Baumgartner	**Hungarian**	18	-	1	20th

THE TEAM

Team principal:	**Paul Stoddart**
Managing director:	**Gian Carlo Minardi**
Technical director:	**Gabriele Tredozi**
Chief designer:	**tba**
Chief engineer:	**Andrew Tilley**
Team manager:	**Massimo Rivola**
Third driver:	**tba**
Chassis:	**Minardi PS05**
Engine:	**Cosworth V10**
Tyres:	**Michelin**

CHRISTIJAN ALBERS

Having tried before to become an F1 driver, Christijan has now quit touring cars in an attempt to fulfil the single-seater dream he has held all his life.

Christijan came close to making his graduation to Formula One in 2003 as part of an all-Dutch line-up alongside Jos Verstappen at Minardi, but the seat that had been earmarked for him went instead to Justin Wilson as promised sponsorship failed to show. Two years on, it wasn't clear as this book closed for press whether Christijan had finally made it to F1, but he tested strongly for both Jordan and Minardi. Indeed he was the fastest of the 10 or more drivers who had a run-out for the Italian team at Misano in November.

Rebuffed by Formula One in 2003, Christijan returned for a further two seasons with Mercedes in the German Touring Car Championship, stepping up from Team Rosberg to the works AMG team and winning four rounds in 2003. He finished third overall last year.

What has tipped the balance in Christijan's favour this time around has been the grouping together of a band of Dutch sponsors anxious to put Formula One back on the country's sporting radar after a year with no one to cheer.

In addition to looking long and hard at Jordan and Minardi, which was natural considering that he raced for team owner Paul Stoddart in Formula 3000 in 2000, he also endeavoured to land a ride in Champ Cars with Walker Racing.

TRACK NOTES

Nationality:	**DUTCH**
Born:	**APRIL 16, 1979, EINDHOVEN, HOLLAND**
Website:	**www.christijan-albers.nl**
Teams:	**MINARDI 2005**
First Grand Prix:	**2005 AUSTRALIAN GP**
Grand Prix starts:	**0**
Grand Prix wins:	**0**
Poles:	**0**
Fastest laps:	**0**
Points:	**0**
Honours:	**2003 GERMAN TOURING CAR RUNNER-UP, 1999 GERMAN FORMULA THREE CHAMPION, 1997 DUTCH FORMULA FORD CHAMPION, 1997 DUTCH INTERCONTINENTAL A KART CHAMPION**

MINARDI NUMBER TWO

The battle to land a ride with Minardi normally involves a huge number of candidates, and this year was no different from usual with as many as 20 drivers vying for the right to line up alongside Christijan Albers.

At the time of going to press just after New Year, the only thing that was clear at the Italian outfit was that Christijan Albers had signed up to lead the team. However, it was by no means certain who would fill the team's second seat. Many said that it would be Zsolt Baumgartner running for a second season with the team after proving steady and consistent rather than rapid in 2004.

But a glance down a ridiculously long list of likelies showed that almost any of them would have a chance, as long as they could land that all important budget which is so essential to keep Paul Stoddart's team going. Many attended a mass test for the team in Italy late last autumn before heading off to chase sponsorship from every quarter over the close-season.

Danish driver Nicolas Kiesa, who raced for the team in the final five grands prix of the 2003

campaign, emerged as one of the favourites. As ever looking to land the most lucrative deal possible, Stoddart famously doesn't like to make his decision on the identity of his drivers until the 11th hour. However, another former Minardi racer, Jos Verstappen, was also thought to be in the running, although many considered that his day has been and gone and that Dutch backers would rather put their money behind a younger driver.

On the list of other hopefuls were not only last year's racer Gianmaria Bruni and last year's Minardi test driver Bas Leinders, but also Renault test driver Franck Montagny who's eager to go racing again. Dropped by Jordan after a troubled campaign in 2004, Italian charger Giorgio Pantano was also mentioned in despatches. Formula 3000 racer Robert Doornbos was in the

mix, although he was tipped to join Jordan, with 2004 rivals Patrick Friesacher and Jeffrey van Hooydonk also in the running.

Sometime Champ Car racer Tiago Monteiro was looking to advance from the Formula Dallara Nissan series, while Neel Jani, Giorgio Mondini, Christian Montanari and Damien Pasini were all hoping to move into the big time from the Formula Renault V6 Championship. Those eager to make the leap from Formula Three included Australian racers Will Davison and Will Power, Poland's Robert Kubica plus Japanese-based Italian Ronnie Quintarelli. With this multi-tude of drivers each paying out small sums of money to have a test run, the vast majority were going to be disappointed, especially as there was always the possibility of someone else emerging to snatch the seat.

NEW SEASON
NEW RULES

It's all change for 2005, with cars having their downforce slashed to slow them. Their engines must also last for two grands prix, all of which gave the teams plenty to think about as they planned for the season ahead.

The enterprising minds of Formula One designers and engineers appear to know no bounds for, every time that they're pinned back by a set of rules aimed at slowing the cars down, they bounce back and their cars go faster still.

When considering the fact that the fastest of the cars in 2004 were slashing up to three seconds off the lap records of most circuits, FIA President Max Mosley decided something had to be done. For example, Minardi qualified faster at this year's Brazilian GP than Ferrari's Rubens Barrichello had lapped to take pole position at the

same venue 18 months earlier, having knocked three seconds off their lap time. With this in mind, Mosley proposed three packages of rule changes and left it to the teams to decide which would be acceptable.

Eventually, the teams opted for the set covering the middle ground, much as Mosley had expected they would. He's not described as a consummate politician for nothing. The package included aerodynamic changes, such as the front wing being raised by 50mm and the cars' rear wing being brought forward by 100mm,

plus the height both of the diffusers and the bodywork ahead of the front wheels being reduced, with the aim of cutting the downforce by 25-30 per cent. Tyres will have to last longer, with one set lasting for the practice sessions on the Friday and Saturday, then a second set that will have to last through qualifying and the whole race. This will restrict pit stops purely to refuelling and mean that a harder rubber compound will have to be used to make tyres last, which, in turn, will slow the cars' progress. Finally, rather than having to last for an entire grand

prix meeting, engines now have to last for two, a move enforced to encourage manufacturers to cut their horsepower to ensure longevity. It's a set of rules that is intended to give the designers and engineers a real challenge. After these proposals, some were saying that although there would be a restriction in downforce, down to 15 per cent by the start of the season, they would be able to catch up completely by the end of the year...

With Jaguar Racing having folded, to be revived as Red Bull Racing, and with both Jordan and Minardi facing up to a bleak winter

battling for survival, keeping costs in check became of even greater interest to the teams. To that end, they sat at the Brazilian GP and agreed on a set of rule amendments for the season ahead. Well, nine of the ten teams did, with Ferrari notable in refusing to sign the document that would have given the teams the unanimity they needed for their changes to go through. This placed Ferrari in the role of the bad guys, but they were merely defending their position of having more money than all of their rivals (with the exception of Toyota) and their desire to test as much as possible, especially on the Bridgestone tyres that are all but tailor-made for them. In short, they didn't want to give up even a

fraction of their advantage to ensure that all teams can afford to continue. However, the fact that their refusal to sign up to the changes could lead to the privateer teams, such as Jordan or Minardi, going to the wall, if not this year then next, should prick their conscience and make them see that desperate times call for desperate measures. Then again, perhaps their six consecutive constructors' championships has made them blind to anything other than winning, winning, winning; blind to the fact that they might, one day, end up racing only themselves.

The changes proposed by the "gang of nine" were that testing should be cut to just ten days per year, but this would be augmented

by two two-hour sessions on the Friday of each grand prix meeting. In return for taking these cuts, the teams would agree to add 18th and 19th races to the calendar, thus bringing the highly-regarded French and British GPs back on board, races that both the teams and their sponsors wanted. There would also be restrictions on the amount of testing carried out by Bridgestone and Michelin on their tyres and a study into the possibility of Formula One running on a single tyre type in the years ahead. Ferrari, though, wanted no restriction on either testing or tyre development. Then again, it's the only team that has its own test track and the only team that has tyres developed specifically for it, so one

Engine failures will be a disaster as they have to last two meetings. Above: teams have agreed to cut testing

can see why it fought its corner.

These changes may be fairly sweeping, but Mosley has bolder ones planned for 2006, including a move away from 3.0-litre V10 engines to 2.4-litre V8s, something that is expected to suit Renault, but which had BMW, Honda and Mercedes up in arms for a while.

Two years after this, in 2008, the year after the current Concorde Agreement that binds the regulations comes to an end, the changes will go further still in order to have cars that cost less – thus attracting more teams to enter – with no driver aids and slick tyres.

KNOW THE TRACKS 2005

With Formula One finding a foothold in Bahrain and China last year, this time around it's time to welcome Turkey and be thankful that a few classic venues have hung on, for now...

For so long, the FIA's Formula One World Championship has been something of a constant with a few fly-away races followed by the bulk of the campaign taking place in Europe, save for a foray to Canada, and then the season has been wrapped up by a few more fly-aways. Now, however, there is set to be a changing of the guard as countries that have held grands prix for decades have found themselves facing the chop to make way for countries beyond the European heartland of old. Tradition stands for nothing when the world's burgeoning markets are to be embraced. So, for a while last autumn, it was a case of welcome Istanbul, and farewell Magny-Cours and Silverstone.

Ringmaster Bernie Ecclestone said that he would love to keep the old along with the new, but the teams stressed that in the interest of keeping costs in check they would put their feet down and race no more than 17 times per season. Last year's 18-round campaign was a one-off, they said.

Negotiations were long and heated but, regardless of the retention of the regular circuits, which was finally agreed in early November, it was always clear that Formula One fans were to be treated to another circuit new to Formula One, new to racing actually: the Istanbul Racing Circuit. If it can match the wonderful facilities that were built from scratch in Bahrain and China for 2004, then it will have done well. The drivers won't welcome the blazing heat that bakes Istanbul at the end of August, although they will be delighted that the soaring temperatures won't be compounded by the soaring humidity that they face in Malaysia.

One of the beauties of Formula One is that no two circuits are alike, although the prevalence of Hermann Tilke – the designer of many new facilities added to the calendar since the Malaysian Grand Prix in 1999 – has made them less different than before. Attend any race and if you only look at the grandstands you will see a world of difference, from the klaxon-blaring Germans to

the face-painted *tifosi* and the fervent, but silent, Japanese. And then, of course, there's the differing styles of blacktop for drivers to race on, plus the ever-changing influence of the weather, something that often puts a whole new slant on things.

This year's schedule falls into a familiar pattern, with Albert Park kicking off proceedings on the first weekend in March. This will be its last time in pole position apparently, but its carnival atmosphere and downtown setting is a jewel in Formula One's crown whatever time of year it has its race. Sepang and Bahrain follow next, sharing the twin hallmarks of circuit designer Tilke's pen and sweltering heat.

The sheer variety of circuits visited by Formula One continues when the circus reaches Europe, starting with Imola, then moving on to the Circuit de Catalunya, which

is in turn light years away from the race after that: Monaco. Indeed no circuit is quite like it, with its steep, narrow streets and its glamorous blast past the yachts along the harbour front.

After a visit to the Nurburgring, the North American double-header of Montreal and Indianapolis could not be more varied in style either and, following that, the purpose-built racing circuits of Magny-Cours, Silverstone and Hockenheim before a trip to the Hungaroring. Next up is the inaugural Turkish Grand Prix at the all-new Istanbul Racing Circuit before a visit to the most long-standing circuit of all, Monza, dating back to 1922.

Then comes Spa-Francorchamps with its fast sweepers in a majestic setting that shows the cars at their very best. Then it's off to Brazil to the pearl of South America's circuits, Interlagos, and on to challenging

Suzuka. The season is rounded out with a second visit to the impressive Shanghai International Circuit, a track blessed with a long straight into a hairpin to help overtaking.

So, that's a record tally of 19 grands prix, up one even on last year's extended campaign. With talk of a Mexican Grand Prix in the pipeline to be held near Cancun as well as a South African one in Cape Town, both on circuits still to be built, there will continue to be pressure on the traditional circuits in Europe, especially as Ecclestone is openly pushing for grands prix both in India and Russia before the decade is out.

Traditionalists shouldn't bewail this change, but acknowledge instead that the new circuits have proved increasingly good, with last year's additions in Bahrain and China showing that circuit designer Tilke is really improving his craft.

MELBOURNE

It's fast, it's sweeping and it's inevitably the venue at which Formula One fans get to see the lie of the land for the year ahead, when it hosts the season's opening race.

To understand sporting passion fully, any fan has to visit Australia. Not only do Australians love sport in its many forms, but they're good at it, too: as was made plain by achieving by far the greatest ratio of gold medals per capita in last autumn's Olympic Games. They offer support with gusto and then some, all of which makes the Australian Grand Prix the ideal race to pull the championship out of its winter of cloak-and-dagger testing and claim and counter-claim about who is competitive. As all racing fans know, when the flag drops, the bullshit stops.

So, Melbourne's Albert Park is a race of revelation. With its first and third corners being 90-degree right-handers, action is assured on the opening lap. After all, who can forget Ralf Schumacher going skywards into Turn 1 in 2002

or Martin Brundle destroying his Jordan at Turn 3 in 1996? All of this is cheered on by fans who lap up not only the grand prix but all the support races and sideshows, too. They turn out to be entertained, to sit in the sunshine and to have a day out of wall-to-wall entertainment.

Snaking around a lake in a once-rundown park just a short distance from the bright lights, restaurants and casino along the banks of the River Yarra, the circuit is generally a mixture of short straights and tight corners as the track keeps turning right, but the back section offers a fabulous sweeping arc between Clark and Waite corners, spitting the hard-triers across the kerbs on its exit before they head through the Hill kink and brake hard for Ascari. Passing may be tricky, but it's far from impossible.

INSIDE TRACK

AUSTRALIAN GRAND PRIX

Date:	**6 March**
Circuit length:	**3.303 miles/5.315km**
Number of laps:	**58**
Lap record:	**M Schumacher (Ferrari), 1m24.125s, 141.016mph/226.933kph, 2004**
Telephone:	**00 61 3 92587100**
Website:	**www.grandprix.com.au**

PREVIOUS WINNERS

1997	**David Coulthard** McLAREN
1998	**Mika Hakkinen** McLAREN
1999	**Eddie Irvine** FERRARI
2000	**Michael Schumacher** FERRARI
2001	**Michael Schumacher** FERRARI
2002	**Michael Schumacher** FERRARI
2003	**David Coulthard** McLAREN
2004	**Michael Schumacher** FERRARI

Ease of access: Frequent buses and trams stop at its gates and it is only a short taxi ride from the heart of the city.

Multi-purpose facility: The track threads its way through a golf course, but a good drive off the first tee on race day would probably end up ricocheting off one of the many catering outlets that are brought in specially for the occasion.

On the beach: After Monaco, the Albert Park circuit is the next closest to the sea, with the beach three blocks from the track.

Local hero: Mark Webber who wowed the crowd with fifth place on his F1 debut here for Minardi in 2002, but they will be expecting more from him with Williams.

Drivers at work: The first corner, Fangio, at which drivers have to carry as much speed as possible without running wide and bouncing over the kerbs, à la Montoya. It's good for outbraking moves, too.

Where to watch: Fangio, Clark Chicane and the slow right called Stewart, two corners before the end of the lap.

David Coulthard's McLaren is dwarfed by the city's skyline as he races to victory in 2003's Australian GP

SEPANG

It's hot and humid, tiring both drivers and pit crews alike, but the Malaysian GP is now well established on the world calendar thanks, largely, to the excellent Sepang circuit.

Burning off the competition, Mika Hakkinen leads the race to the first corner on the opening lap in 2000

Just fly in: It might be 30km from Kuala Lumpur, but Sepang is right next to the airport and is linked to both by a new railway line as well as by motorway.

Contrasting capital: Kuala Lumpur has the world's tallest building, the startling Petronas Twin Towers, on the one hand and the tumbledown Chinese market, home of replica everything, on the other.

Waiting for a hero: Malaysian fans have been longing for a driver of their own to cheer to glory, but Alex Yoong who turned out for Minardi in 2002 proved less than rapid, so they're still waiting.

Keep your cool: The 40-degree heat and soaring humidity are draining.

Drink up: Their nutritionists concoct a special isoponic brew that drivers suck through a pipe into their helmet to counteract the 40-degree heat.

Drivers at work: The fourth corner, Langkawi, is the toughest. It's a second gear right-hander approached at 180mph.

Where to watch: The final corner and the first/second corner complex, as this is where the overtaking happens.

There are some who worry that Hermann Tilke designs seemingly every circuit new to Formula One, such as Bahrain and Shanghai, but they should have no concerns about Sepang as it's his best. Why so? Because it offers places at which cars can overtake. The key is to have a long straight feeding into a tight corner, especially with the track being five cars wide at the turn-in point. And Sepang has two such corners: one leading into the final corner of the lap, leading onto the start/finish straight, and the other at the far end of that straight, at the first corner. Small wonder, then, that the grandstand's seats there are highly prized.

There's another reason why any grandstand seat at Sepang should be coveted: they're all under cover, offering shade that is all but essential in the scorching conditions. For anyone emerging from a European winter to contemplate watching the race without shade overhead would be madness. Also, going for a stroll to other vantage points around the sinuous track's perimeter might offer the chance to meet the least friendly locals: the snakes... Mind you, it might just be worth it in order to watch how brave the drivers are in the tricky Langkawi bend, the fourth corner of the lap. Yet, Tilke's massive grandstands offer you the view of half of the lap, a treat unrivalled at any other venue now that the A1-ring has dropped off the calendar.

Into Turn 1 is a favourite, as shown at the start every year. But Turn 2 follows swiftly and Jarno Trulli will recall that he was assaulted by Michael Schumacher there in 2003.

BAHRAIN

 New to the World Championship last year, Bahrain made an impression, with its excellent new circuit augmented by an insight into the Arab world: a culture entirely new to F1.

Bahrain is a worthy country, a trading nation on the Arabian Gulf, but, in terms of prestige, it lags behind neighbouring Dubai. Brash in comparison, Dubai has long hosted world-class sporting events, such as powerboating, golf and tennis, to spread its name around the world. Then, last year, Bahrain played its trump card and hosted a grand prix, outstripping all that had gone on in Dubai over a decade and more. The ugly duckling had turned into a swan.

The ingredients didn't sound that promising: Hermann Tilke, the designer, had to scratch a circuit out of a patch of desert at Sakhir to the south of the capital, Manama. As is the case with all of Tilke's circuits, the emphasis, out of deference to the safety standards required, is on tight and technical, but he was given the money (£83m) to ensure that everything was finished to standards that would make the management at Silverstone green with envy.

The circuit is divided into two distinct parts: one characterising the desert and the other an oasis, with sprinklers keeping the grass verges verdant in the section of track close to the pits, paddock and grandstands. The desert section comes after the tight first corner, with the track twisting its way through rocky hillocks until it reaches the back straight, where it re-enters the oasis section which it quits at Turn 11 for a run through more desert until the corner onto the start/finish straight and yet more green verges.

For all the investment, however, there were problems at the inaugural event: the desert looked more like rubble than the pristine sand dunes imagined by first-time visitors. In addition, the stones on the inside of the kerbs were sharp rather than rounded. Despite the fact that they had been sprayed with glue, they were fired onto the track by errant cars during the race and this led to numerous punctures.

INSIDE TRACK

BAHRAIN GRAND PRIX

Date:	**3 April**
Circuit length:	**3.366 miles/5.417km**
Number of laps:	**57**
Lap record:	**M Schumacher (Ferrari), 1m30.252s, 134.260mph/216.061kph, 2004**
Telephone:	**00 973 406222**
Website:	**www.bahraingp.com.bh**

PREVIOUS WINNERS

2004	**Michael Schumacher** FERRARI

Island hopping: Bahrain is made up of 36 islands, with a total area of 706 square kilometres. Bahrain island is 48km long and 16km wide.

Unusual neighbours: Bahrain Circuit is located next to a camel farm.

New for 2005: The stony areas inside the kerbs that caused problems in 2004 have been replaced by Astroturf.

Only little: With a population of 620,000, Bahrain is the third least-populous country to host a grand prix after San Marino (27,000) and Monaco (34,000).

Make it a holiday: Dubai hosts its sporting events not just for prestige but also for the tourists, and Bahrain is boosting its tourism infrastructure to follow suit.

Seats to spare: Not all the grandstands were full for the 2004 race, something explained by the fact that Sunday is a working day in Bahrain.

It could be hot: Last year's race-day temperature was 30°C, but qualifying had been in temperatures of 50-plus.

Drivers at work: The left-right-left esses after Turn 5.

Where to watch: From the ten-storey tower if you're a VIP; this offers views of the entire circuit. However, if you're a mere mortal interested in outbraking manoeuvres, then go to the first corner.

Midnight at the Oasis: no expense has been spared in the construction of Bahrain's fabulous desert track

IMOLA

Outdated Imola has made it through another winter, keeping its place in the World Championship. For this, Formula One fans should rejoice, for the track has soul.

Five-time winner at Imola, Michael Schumacher blasts past in a blur of speed on his way to victory in 2004

INSIDE TRACK

SAN MARINO GRAND PRIX

Date:	**24 April**
Circuit length:	**3.064 miles/4.930km**
Number of laps:	**62**
Lap record:	**M Schumacher (Ferrari), 1m20.411s, 137.230mph/220.840kph, 2004**
Telephone:	**00 39 0542 34116**
Website:	**www.autodromoimola.com**

PREVIOUS WINNERS

1995	**Damon Hill** WILLIAMS
1996	**Damon Hill** WILLIAMS
1997	**Heinz-Harald Frentzen** WILLIAMS
1998	**David Coulthard** McLAREN
1999	**Michael Schumacher** FERRARI
2000	**Michael Schumacher** FERRARI
2001	**Ralf Schumacher** WILLIAMS
2002	**Michael Schumacher** FERRARI
2003	**Michael Schumacher** FERRARI
2004	**Michael Schumacher** FERRARI

Not in San Marino: It may be called the San Marino Grand Prix, but the race is actually held in Italy rather than in the mountainous principality. Imola is 33km south-east of Bologna.

What's in a name?: Imola is in Ferrari country. Its full name is the Autodromo Enzo e Dino Ferrari in tribute to the Ferrari founder's son Dino, who died of illness in his 30s.

Going for six: Victory for Michael Schumacher will give the seven-time world champion four Imola wins in succession and six in all.

Drivers at work: A good line over the kerbs at Variante Alta helps a driver to carry speed down the kinked straight to Rivazza. A bad one forces them to make an unwanted lift off the throttle.

Where to watch: The views from Tosa and Acque Minerali are beautiful, but the best place to watch the race is at Rivazza.

With Bernie Ecclestone looking to spread the Formula One gospel to the four corners of the world, but with the team bosses wanting to keep a cap of 17 or 18 races per season, it looked as though Imola's days as a grand prix venue were numbered. Somehow, though, this charming Italian circuit has survived for another year.

The arrival of the new circuits in Bahrain and China last year raised the bar in terms of what is expected, and their facilities make Imola look outmoded - an anachronism with its tiny pit garages, narrow pitlane and cramped paddock. Yet, Imola has something that the new kids on the Formula One block do not have: history. And now it has a contract through to 2009.

The other point that made the future of the San Marino Grand Prix look decidedly shaky is that it's one of two races held in Italy, something of a luxury at a time when Ecclestone wants to spread Formula One away from Europe.

For all its tiring facilities, this pretty venue is still a wonderful place to watch Formula One cars in action as they race through the parkland, hopefully in the soft sunlight of an Italian spring. The view as they crest the hill at Piratella and tumble down to the dip at Acque Minerali is fabulous, as is the chicane at Variante Alta. For Ferrari fans, who make up the vast majority, the most heart-warming sight is the hillside between Variante Bassa and the start/finish straight, awash as it is with flags showing allegiance to the marque's Prancing Horse.

BARCELONA

 Unless it was motorbike racing, the Circuit de Catalunya used to struggle to fill the stands. Since the arrival of new national hero Fernando Alonso, they've had to enlarge them...

The fans rise to Michael Schumacher as he takes the chequered flag to make it five wins in a row last year

INSIDE TRACK

SPANISH GRAND PRIX

Date:	8 May
Circuit length:	2.939 miles/4.730km
Number of laps:	66
Lap record:	M Schumacher (Ferrari), 1m17.450s, 133.644mph/215.069kph, 2004
Telephone:	00 34 93 5719771
Website:	www.circuitcat.com

PREVIOUS WINNERS

1995	Michael Schumacher	BENETTON
1996	Michael Schumacher	FERRARI
1997	Jacques Villeneuve	WILLIAMS
1998	Mika Hakkinen	McLAREN
1999	Mika Hakkinen	McLAREN
2000	Mika Hakkinen	McLAREN
2001	Michael Schumacher	FERRARI
2002	Michael Schumacher	FERRARI
2003	Michael Schumacher	FERRARI
2004	Michael Schumacher	FERRARI

Handy for the city: The Circuit de Catalunya is situated just beyond the northern suburbs of Barcelona. You can reach Montmelo by car or by train.

Third time lucky: Barcelona has hosted grands prix at two other circuits, namely the Pedralbes street circuit and later the track in Montjuic Park, home to the 1992 Olympic stadium. This venue lost its race after 1975, when Rolf Stommelen flew over a barrier and killed four spectators.

Something for everyone: The circuit is excellent for testing because it has a mixture of fast and slow corners.

Drivers at work: Renault, the third corner, where the drivers have to guide their cars through this 150-degree uphill right-hander.

Where to watch: Elf, the first corner at the end of the longest straight in Formula One, where first-lap action is almost guaranteed.

Spain is still waiting for its first world champion; a weak record considering that it is a country with a population of 40 million and that it has been hosting grands prix since as long ago as 1913 and rounds of the World Championship since 1951. In Fernando Alonso, though, they may finally have the driver to bring them the success they crave.

So, with crowds finally pouring through the turnstiles, have they got a circuit worthy of their expectations? Yes, indeed they have - the Circuit de Catalunya is something of a treat. Not only does it possess the longest straight on the Formula One calendar, but it also feeds into a tight esses, something that ought to all but guarantee overtaking. However, that is something that will only happen again when the rules have been changed to reduce aerodynamics, so

that a driver can get close enough to the car it is chasing through the fast final corner to enable a tow past the pits. Until that happens, the "dirty", turbulent air from the leading car will make overtaking in this way difficult.

This, the fifth home of the Spanish Grand Prix, is a track that offers few surprises to the teams as the majority of them use it as their principal test circuit. However, wind is a major factor here and this can throw a whole new set of variables at the teams and car set-up here still requires a certain amount of guesswork.

The lap holds many tricky corners for the drivers; with the line over the blind brow at Campsa a crucial factor when it comes to speed down the back straight. The position drivers take into La Caixa corner, which was re-profiled for last year, is also of vital importance.

MONTE CARLO

In a world in which ancient is often replaced by modern, the Monaco Grand Prix remains an anachronism, but its narrow streets and stunning harbour make it the jewel in F1's crown.

Walk around Monte Carlo 51 weeks of the year and you would have no idea that a Formula One grand prix could possibly be held there. The streets are impossibly narrow and the harbourside is more of a promenade than a circuit.

However, remove the parked cars, erect the barriers and you can almost accept that it's possible. It's hard to believe that drivers are able to top 160mph up the hill to Casino Square, but race they do and they have done since 1929. The image of Monte Carlo as a playground for the rich remains, with the casino and the harbour full of yachts that cost well over seven figures.

It comes as no surprise, then, that the celebrities love to be seen here. The circuit itself is a squeeze from the start/finish straight that isn't straight to the constriction of the first corner, Ste Devote, all the way around to the reprofiled Piscine section. It's bumpy, too.

With barriers lining its length, it demands concentration. The preferential status conferred on the circuit by the sponsors has meant that, while other tracks have had to be modified, Monaco's circuit has lagged behind. Finally, though, the teams' voices were heard and the introduction of a new pit complex last year was the biggest improvement in aeons, offering the pit garages and even team offices that are taken for granted elsewhere.

Last year's race demonstrated the darker side of the tunnel. First, there was the incident where Fernando Alonso swerved to avoid Ralf Schumacher and thumped into the barriers. Then there was the Michael Schumacher/Juan Pablo Montoya collision behind the resultant safety car. Coping with bright light into dark and then accelerating up to 180mph is hard enough without meeting an obstacle...

INSIDE TRACK

MONACO GRAND PRIX

Date:	**22 May**
Circuit length:	**2.075 miles/3.339km**
Number of laps:	**78**
Lap record:	**M Schumacher (Ferrari), 1m14.439s, 100.373mph/161.527kph, 2004**
Telephone:	**00 377 93152600**
Website:	**www.acm.mc**

PREVIOUS WINNERS

1995	**Michael Schumacher**	BENETTON
1996	**Olivier Panis**	LIGIER
1997	**Michael Schumacher**	FERRARI
1998	**Mika Hakkinen**	McLAREN
1999	**Michael Schumacher**	FERRARI
2000	**David Coulthard**	McLAREN
2001	**Michael Schumacher**	FERRARI
2002	**David Coulthard**	McLAREN
2003	**Juan Pablo Montoya**	WILLIAMS
2004	**Jarno Trulli**	RENAULT

Save up your pennies: If you really want to impress, make sure you book a suite at The Hermitage, where the balconies overlook the climb to Casino Square.

With royal approval: Monaco's podium is guaranteed to have a royal presence. The Grimaldi family - rulers of Monaco since 1297 - are always there when the trophies are handed out.

Still waiting: Ayrton Senna won at Monaco every year from 1989 to 1993. Michael Schumacher still needs one more victory to equal Senna's record of six wins in the principality.

Drivers at work: Getting the line right through Massenet determines a driver's speed into Casino Square. The entry is blind and the barriers are close at hand.

Where to watch: The exit of Casino Square for spectacle or Nouvelle Chicane for overtaking moves as they hit the harbour front.

The new pits have offices that look down to the stretch of circuit after Piscine and even garages below

NURBURGRING

Germany's first taste of Formula One every year comes with a race billed as the European GP around the twists and recently modified turns of the Nurburgring track in the Eifel mountains

If ever a circuit was damned by its past, then the Nurburgring is it. It's a perfectly acceptable modern venue, but the fact that the original Nurburgring Nordschleife, all 14-plus miles of it, lurks in the background, makes it pale into insignificance. That the European Grand Prix is held on the modern circuit gives credence to calls for it to be dropped from the calendar in order to make way for new flyaway races. After all, it's a second German Grand Prix under a title of convenience. However, with Schumacher sweeping all before him, the grandstands will always be packed...

Despite holding on to its traditional slot at the end of May, the European GP may yet be given a sting in the tail as the Eifel mountains have a microclimate of their own and rain can come at a moment's notice to liven proceedings. After all, changing weather in 1999 led to Johnny Herbert giving Stewart its only win.

Hermann Tilke made his mark several years ago by changing the first corner esses that often left drivers bouncing through the gravel for the Mercedes Arena that starts with a sharp hairpin feeding into a pair of lightly banked left-handers and a right before dipping down to the sweeping Ford Kurve as before.

If it's spectacle you seek, look to the left-right chicane on the back straight where, in 2003, drivers were prevented from running over the kerbs, as was shown when Fernando Alonso realized that his car wouldn't go around the corner as intended, braked early and left David Coulthard with no option but to crash in avoidance.

Local hero Michael Schumacher drives himself round the bend during a practice session at the Nurburgring

MONTREAL

Now part of an eminently sensible North American double-header, the Montreal circuit ought to have its place firmly cemented into the calendar because everyone loves it.

The Circuit Gilles Villeneuve with its stunning backdrop of the St Lawrence River and the Montreal skyline

Perhaps the Circuit Gilles Villeneuve on an island in the St Lawrence River in Montreal isn't the greatest strip of blacktop in the world to drive. It certainly falls a long way short of Spa-Francorchamps and Suzuka in terms of driving challenge, as basically it is a pair of hairpins joined together by a handful of sweepers and a chicane that provide more of a test on a car's brakes and transmission. Add to that the fact that the teams have to operate in a cramped environment that scarcely offers a paddock behind their pit garages and you would wonder why the track is so popular with drivers, teams and certainly the fans. The reason is simple: Montreal is a dynamic, fun city that offers a rare chance for a little social life, in much the same way as Melbourne at the start of the season. Put

simply, it's a happy trade-off. Formula One needs to go to cities from time to time to take its excitement to the people to turn them into devotees.

Although you can see the skyscrapers of downtown Montreal from almost any point on the circuit, the fact that the race is staged on an island on the far side of a broad river means that there is a clear separation. Used to host the Expo '67 exhibition, the Ile de Notre Dame is long and thin and offers little space for the facilities required, with the rowing lake used when Montreal hosted the 1976 Olympics running behind the pits all the way up to the L'Epingle hairpin, the spot where Nigel Mansell so famously threw away victory on the final lap in 1991 by waving to the fans before his engine cut out.

INSIDE TRACK

CANADIAN GRAND PRIX

Date:	**12 June**
Circuit length:	**2.710 miles/4.361km**
Number of laps:	**70**
Lap record:	**R Barrichello (Ferrari), 1m13.622s, 132.511mph/213.246kph, 2004**
Telephone:	**001 514 350 0000**
Website:	**www.grandprix.ca**

PREVIOUS WINNERS

1995	**Jean Alesi** FERRARI
1996	**Damon Hill** WILLIAMS
1997	**Michael Schumacher** FERRARI
1998	**Michael Schumacher** FERRARI
1999	**Mika Hakkinen** McLAREN
2000	**Michael Schumacher** FERRARI
2001	**Ralf Schumacher** WILLIAMS
2002	**Michael Schumacher** FERRARI
2003	**Michael Schumacher** FERRARI
2004	**Michael Schumacher** FERRARI

What's in a name?: The circuit was named after Gilles Villeneuve, who was the winner of the first Canadian GP held here in 1978 after the race was moved from Mosport Park.

Arrive by metro: As is the case with Albert Park in Melbourne, the circuit can be reached by public transport. There is a metro station just by its entrance.

What are those flags?: The blue-and-white flags are the flags of Quebec, Villeneuve's home province.

Drivers at work: The chicane onto the start/finish straight is tricky. The wall on the exit proved almost magnetic to world champions in 1999 as Damon Hill, Michael Schumacher and Jacques Villeneuve all hit it.

Where to watch: The whole complex from the left-hander at the end of the start/finish straight to the exit of the long right that follows.

INDIANAPOLIS

The home of American motorsport, the Indianapolis Motor Speedway has played host to the United States Grand Prix since it was revived in 2000. It always provides a spectacle.

Ralf Schumacher will be feeling more than a little trepidation as he faces the return to the Indianapolis Motor Speedway this June, for its concrete walls proved that they could bite last season - the back injuries that he suffered from his 78g impact with them kept him out for much of the rest of the season.

The walls are a major feature of the circuit, but only along the banked section, while the twisting infield into which it feeds offers grass verges, gravel beds and tyre barriers like any other modern venue. Formula One uses a combination of a new circuit around the infield plus the start/finish straight and some of Turns 1 and 2, albeit in reverse direction. The first corner is tight as the cars feed off the start/finish straight onto the infield with a series of twists until a right-hander feeds onto a back straight. It is a lap of two distinct parts, but at least both offer an opportunity to overtake at the end of their longest straight, which is more than can be said for some of the other venues.

No visitor can fail to be blown away by the sheer scale of the place: its massive grandstands surround one straight and both banked corners of the full, 2.5-mile oval. Indeed, the scale is made plain by the fact that Turns 3 and 4 can be seen from the grandstands at Turns 1 and 2 but are fully a mile away... When the grandstands are filled for the annual Indy 500 and the Brickyard 400 race for NASCAR stock cars, it is a sight to behold.

INSIDE TRACK

UNITED STATES GRAND PRIX

Date:	**19 June**
Circuit length:	**2.606 miles/4.195km**
Number of laps:	**73**
Lap record:	**R Barrichello (Ferrari), 1m10.399s, 133.207mph/214.366kph, 2004**
Telephone:	**001 317 481 8500**
Website:	**www.my.brickyard.com**

PREVIOUS WINNERS

2000	**Michael Schumacher**	FERRARI
2001	**Mika Hakkinen**	McLAREN
2002	**Rubens Barrichello**	FERRARI
2003	**Michael Schumacher**	FERRARI
2004	**Michael Schumacher**	FERRARI

Go west: The Motor Speedway is located in the city's western suburbs.

Sporting variety: If you fancy action on some smaller ovals, the nearby circuits at Indiana State Fairground and Indy Raceway Park have full programmes over race weekend.

It's huge: The Indianapolis Motor Speedway can seat 350,000 spectators in its grandstands, with a reduced capacity for the grand prix.

A race on the move: The United States Grand Prix has been held at five different circuits - Sebring, Riverside, Watkins Glen and Phoenix as well as Indianapolis.

Drivers at work: Turn 11, the right-hander where the infield feeds back onto the banking between Turns 2 and 1, where a good entry might yield that all-important tow down the straight.

Where to watch: Turns 1 and 2, the right-left esse off the main straight that is approached at 200mph where a wide track funnels into a narrow one, leading to inevitable clashes as two into one does not go, as proved by Juan Pablo Montoya and Rubens Barrichello in 2003.

The immense grandstands are packed as the cars on the grid line up to race. Note the extra-wide pitlane

MAGNY-COURS

Some say F1 cars should either race on great circuits or on street venues. In this case, Magny-Cours would be left out in the cold, but it is still a circuit that provides plenty of incident.

Coulthard and Montoya chase Jenson Button through the Lycee sequence during last year's French GP

Poor Magny-Cours is unloved. It has been regarded as Formula One's bastard son since its government-assisted transformation from a club racing circuit into the home of the French Grand Prix. A stopping-off place for the World Championship since 1991, it has won few friends, despite its modern facilities and huge paddock. Some say that is because there are no decent hotels in this extremely rural area for the teams to stay in – definitely a minus point with the sport's hierarchy – others say that the circuit has no atmosphere. This is a somewhat harsh criticism: although there certainly is little atmosphere as the cows in the neighbouring fields chomp on, unaware of what all the fuss is about, the twisting and bucking blacktop has thrown up plenty of excitement over the intervening years. Anyone lucky enough to have watched the race at the Adelaide hairpin will

attest to that; as the cars arrive in a slipstreaming bunch, the question remains as to who will dare to be last one to hit the brakes.

The trouble comes with the recent changes to the final sequence of corners, the old chicane and Lycee: they have broken the flow of an already interrupted track.

However, these changes are balanced by the wonderful start to the lap in which the drivers have to get their line right through Grande Courbe and the Estoril bend that follows. The downhill Nurburgring esses are pretty fun, too. The engineers find Magny-Cours a challenge as it contains corners of every type, but they love its smooth-playing surface.

Magny-Cours came close to being dropped from last year's calendar, but a cash injection from the regional council saved it. For now, it's back on track.

INSIDE TRACK

FRENCH GRAND PRIX

Date:	**3 July**
Circuit length:	**2.741 miles/4.411km**
Number of laps:	**70**
Lap record:	**M Schumacher (Ferrari), 1m15.377s, 130.910mph/210.669kph, 2004**
Telephone:	**00 33 3 86218000**
Website:	**www.magny-cours.com**

PREVIOUS WINNERS

1995	**Michael Schumacher** BENETTON
1996	**Damon Hill** WILLIAMS
1997	**Michael Schumacher** FERRARI
1998	**Michael Schumacher** FERRARI
1999	**Heinz-Harald Frentzen** JORDAN
2000	**David Coulthard** McLAREN
2001	**Michael Schumacher** FERRARI
2002	**Michael Schumacher** FERRARI
2003	**Ralf Schumacher** WILLIAMS
2004	**Michael Schumacher** FERRARI

In the country: Magny-Cours is a long way from any major city, with Paris 250km to the north.

A long history: France held the first-ever grand prix at Le Mans in 1906, with Magny-Cours' first in 1991.

Seven wins: Michael Schumacher has won the French Grand Prix a record seven times – in 1994, 1995, 1997, 1998, 2001, 2002 and last year.

Something to see: If you have time to kill here, try the museum on the outside of the circuit by Chateau d'Eau corner.

Drivers at work: Estoril provides the greatest challenge as the drivers have to fight negative camber in attempting to achieve the highest exit speed possible to take on to the long back straight.

Where to watch: The Imola esses, as not only are they spectacular when the drivers bounce over them, but you can also see across to the Adelaide hairpin.

SILVERSTONE

 Silverstone's tenure of the British Grand Prix came under pressure last year, many think unfairly, but this great circuit stays on the calendar, to the relief of teams, drivers and fans.

For years, it's seemed that Formula One impresario Bernie Ecclestone has had it in for Silverstone, with constant threats to drop the race and even to replace it with a race around the streets of London. This didn't upset just British fans but also fans the world over concerned by the potential loss of one of the sport's great circuits, the venue of the first-ever round of the F1 World Championship when it kicked off in 1950. The race's future is now secure after the owners of the circuit signed a five-year deal with Ecclestone, through to 2009, which frees the way for government investment to boost the coffers. Not only will there be a new pit and paddock complex but Silverstone is set to become an all-round centre of excellence.

Silverstone is loved by the teams – six of whom are based in England – because it is close to home and, therefore, a race that their backroom staff can attend. The drivers like it too, as its sweepers offer a real challenge. Indeed, anyone who fails to be impressed by the drivers' craft and the cars' adhesion through Becketts has a heart of stone.

Silverstone doesn't stand still, as shown by its many changes in shape over the past two decades, and plans are in place for a new pits complex to be built on the straight after Club Corner. The circuit layout produces overtaking aplenty too, as shown in 2003 when there was passing galore as Rubens Barrichello fought his way to the front. Copse is one such passing place, while the entry to Stowe, the Abbey chicane and through Bridge all offer opportunities.

INSIDE TRACK

BRITISH GRAND PRIX

Date:	10 July
Circuit length:	3.194 miles/5.140km
Number of laps:	60
Lap record:	M Schumacher (Ferrari), 1m18.739s, 146.059mph/235.048kph, 2004
Telephone:	01327 857271
Website: www.silverstone-circuit.co.uk	

PREVIOUS WINNERS

1995	**Johnny Herbert** BENETTON
1996	**Jacques Villeneuve** WILLIAMS
1997	**Jacques Villeneuve** WILLIAMS
1998	**Michael Schumacher** FERRARI
1999	**David Coulthard** McLAREN
2000	**David Coulthard** McLAREN
2001	**Mika Hakkinen** McLAREN
2002	**Michael Schumacher** FERRARI
2003	**Rubens Barrichello** FERRARI
2004	**Michael Schumacher** FERRARI

Easy access: Silverstone is located 25km south-west of Northampton. Traffic queues, once a major problem, have been vanquished by access roads off the recently built A43 bypass around Silverstone village.

Mind the Bridge: Jarno Trulli proved that the circuit can bite last year when his Renault appeared to break at Bridge, pitching him into the barriers at 160mph.

A long history: The circuit was built on a World War Two airfield, opening in 1948.

Unwanted visitor: Let's hope there is no repeat of last year's lunatic track invader who broke onto the Hangar Straight.

Drivers at work: The Becketts esses rank among the toughest corners tackled by F1, with the drivers having to turn in at 155mph and steer right-left-right.

Where to watch: Becketts in qualifying and Stowe during the race, to enjoy the overtaking.

Thousands of fans enjoy a grandstand view of David Coulthard and Ralf Schumacher at Stowe in 2002

HOCKENHEIM

 Last year was the year that the chopped Hockenheim circuit found its feet, proving the revisions had not removed all of the overtaking opportunities at the home of the German GP.

Michael Schumacher beats his brother Ralf into the first corner at Hockenheim in the 2003 German GP

It still takes some time to adjust when you consider Hockenheim. It is four years since the circuit was shorn of its long, 220mph blasts through the forest; these were replaced by a tight right and a long sweeper to a hairpin before the track twists its way back to the stadium section via a right kink, a tight left and a 90-degree right on a lap shortened by 1.5 miles, but the memories of the great races on the previous track are such that one hopes to find it still there. It isn't. Trees are starting to spring up on the old straights, thus consigning the spot where Jim Clark perished in a Formula Two race in 1968 to a more silent future.

Amazingly, for a circuit that was said to lack character when the German Grand Prix decamped there for good from the Nurburgring Nordschleife in 1977 after a one-off visit in 1970, it is widely missed. Fortunately, there was enough action in last year's grand prix to make you think that Hermann Tilke's reworked circuit may be able to entertain the spectators after all.

The stadium section that snakes its way past the grandstands is still intimidating, especially as the field spills into the first corner on the opening lap, an accident never far away. The opportunities at the hairpin can be good too, as shown by Takuma Sato when he passed Jarno Trulli there last year, or Jenson Button's numerous attempts to do the same to Fernando Alonso. Considering how many grands prix Michael Schumacher has won in the past decade, his hit rate at Hockenheim is poor. He has only won the race three times – in 1995, 2002 and last year – but the support for him, unsurprisingly, remains huge.

INSIDE TRACK

GERMAN GRAND PRIX

Date:	**24 July**
Circuit length:	**2.842 miles/4.574km**
Number of laps:	**67**
Lap record:	**K Raikkonen (McLaren), 1m14.917s, 138.685mph/223.471kph, 2004**
Telephone:	**00 49 6205 95005**
Website:	**www.hockenheimring.de**

PREVIOUS WINNERS

1995	**Michael Schumacher**	BENETTON
1996	**Damon Hill**	WILLIAMS
1997	**Gerhard Berger**	BENETTON
1998	**Mika Hakkinen**	McLAREN
1999	**Eddie Irvine**	FERRARI
2000	**Rubens Barrichello**	FERRARI
2001	**Ralf Schumacher**	WILLIAMS
2002	**Michael Schumacher**	FERRARI
2003	**Juan Pablo Montoya**	WILLIAMS
2004	**Michael Schumacher**	FERRARI

Convenient history: To visit Hockenheim, fly in to Frankfurt and stay in the ancient university town of Heidelberg, less than 20 miles north of the circuit.

Fireworks and air horns: The stadium section of the circuit is gladiatorial in feel: more than 100,000 fans let off fireworks, sound air-horns and go berserk whenever a Schumacher hoves into view.

As it was: To understand how the circuit evolved, visit the circuit museum behind the grandstands on the start/finish straight.

Drivers at work: The corner turning into the stadium, the Mobil 1 Kurve, a 90-degree right with an all but blind entry that offers a seemingly wide exit that coaxes many a driver to over commit.

Where to watch: The Spitzkehre, the tight hairpin at the far end of the circuit, approached by a long, long, curving stretch of track.

HUNGARORING

 If fans had to name the dullest track visited by Formula One, the Hungaroring would be it, as its endless, tight curves offer next to no chance of making a passing manoeuvre.

It's simple really: everyone apart from the driver who qualifies on pole position curses the track, for the simple fact that they know they are going to see a processional race. Sure, everyone enjoys visiting the wonderful and historic city of Budapest, but that's not reason enough for Formula One to keep the Hungarian Grand Prix on the calendar. Sadly, Formula One impresario Bernie Ecclestone has just extended the circuit's deal to host the race from 2006 to 2011, so we're stuck with it.

It seems a long time ago, 1986 in fact, when the Hungarian Grand Prix became Formula One's brave new world, its first visit behind the Iron Curtain. Young fans of today won't be aware of the importance of this, but it was breaking new ground, taking the sport's flagship formula to a whole new audience. The world has moved on, however, and it's no longer big news. In truth, its impact has reduced and the facilities just aren't up to scratch, not least that all-important stretch of tarmac on which the drivers go out to race. Yes, the point is, bar a brave move into the first corner on the opening lap, they're able to do little more than follow the car in front and hope that they can pass them by having a superior pit strategy.

Had the circuit been of a more open design, the Hungaroring could have been one of the best, because the track sits in a natural amphitheatre, affording an amazing view for spectators on either side of the valley. All they can see for now, however, is the cars running nose-to-tail for most of the lap. It's a shame.

INSIDE TRACK

HUNGARIAN GRAND PRIX

Date:	**31 July**
Circuit length:	**2.722 miles/4.381km**
Number of laps:	**70**
Lap record:	**M Schumacher (Ferrari), 1m19.071s, 123.945mph/199.461kph, 2004**
Telephone:	**00 36 2 844 1861**
Website:	**www.hungaroring.hu**

PREVIOUS WINNERS

1995	**Damon Hill**	WILLIAMS
1996	**Jacques Villeneuve**	WILLIAMS
1997	**Jacques Villeneuve**	WILLIAMS
1998	**Michael Schumacher**	FERRARI
1999	**Mika Hakkinen**	McLAREN
2000	**Mika Hakkinen**	McLAREN
2001	**Michael Schumacher**	FERRARI
2002	**Rubens Barrichello**	FERRARI
2003	**Fernando Alonso**	RENAULT
2004	**Michael Schumacher**	FERRARI

A wonderful city: Budapest is the place to stay, with the twin cities of Buda and Pest sitting on opposite banks of the Danube.

A sell-out debut: More than 200,000 fans turned out to watch the inaugural grand prix at the Hungaroring in 1986 when Nelson Piquet won for Brabham.

Stifling heat: Drivers need to be well hydrated as the Hungarian GP tends to be the hottest of the European season.

Driving a wide car: Thierry Boutsen's victory for Williams in 1990 was a classic case of keeping cool at the head of a queue for every lap of the race, despite serious pressure from Ayrton Senna.

Drivers at work: Turn 4, as the track climbs the far side of the valley, is where the drivers really have to hang on to maintain speed and position for Turn 5.

Where to watch: The first corner, as this is the only place where you're likely to see overtaking, other than in the pits...

Into the first corner, Michael Schumacher leads team-mate Rubens Barrichello et al at the start in 2004

ISTANBUL

This year's new venue is Turkey, with the Istanbul Racing Circuit ready to offer the drivers a fresh challenge on an all-new track in some of the hottest conditions of the year.

The race to get ready for business is shown by this aerial view of the construction of the all-new circuit

INSIDE TRACK

TURKISH GRAND PRIX

Date:	**21 August**
Circuit length:	**3.293 miles/5.299km**
Number of laps:	**58**
Lap record:	**Not applicable**
Telephone:	**tba**
Website:	**www.formula1-istanbul.com**

East and west: Turkey holds the rare distinction of being both in Europe and in Asia, with the small area of land west of the Bosphorus river that divides Istanbul being in Europe.

What's in a name?: Istanbul was known as Byzantium when it was founded in 660BC before it changed its name to Constantinople in the year 330 and latterly to its current moniker.

Find some shade: It's bound to be hot when Formula One comes to town, so all race-goers would be well advised to book a seat under cover. As many as 75,000 grandstand seats are to be built.

In for the long run: The Turkish government has signed a contract to host a grand prix through until 2011.

Son of his father: The moving force behind the Turkish GP, Mumtaz Tahincioglu, President of the Turkish Automobile Federation, has his eye on one of Turkey's up-and-coming drivers, Jason Tahinci, as he's Jason's father...

One to watch: Turkey's highest-ranked young star is Can Artam who raced in Formula 3000 last year. He's sure to have his sights set on Formula One.

Drivers at work: The trickiest looking stretch of the circuit, judging by its design rather than prior experience, is the quadruple-apex left-hander that follows the hairpin halfway around the lap.

Where to watch: The corner at the end of the kinked back straight, as it offers the most obvious overtaking opportunity.

In Formula One's quest to cast aside some of its traditional and long-established European venues so that it can spread its wings across the globe, Turkey has become the latest country deemed suitable to hold a round of the coveted World Championship. As shown by Turkey's major efforts to join the European Union, the shift away from the European heartland hasn't been excessive. However, in Turkey Formula One impresario Bernie Ecclestone has found another government willing to stump up the cash to build a brand new circuit with all of the features and facilities now deemed de rigueur to land a grand prix.

Hewn out of rocky ground near Pendik some 30 miles east of the country's business centre, Istanbul, the new circuit is yet another from the pen of circuit designer Hermann Tilke. Unusually, this 16-corner circuit runs in an anti-clockwise direction, with a sharp left-hander to start the lap. The track that follows from there is generally twisting and medium speed, save for a kinked back straight down which the cars ought to hit 200mph before reaching the final sequence of corners. This contains a tight left-hander, where there's sure to be overtaking, and then a tight right and a tight left.

It was thought originally that a country such as Turkey, being outside Europe, would be handy for continuing to run cars in the liveries of tobacco sponsors, but the government has vetoed that. However, the government is still keen to host the race as it reckons that resultant tourism will make the expenditure more than worthwhile.

MONZA

 Classic Silverstone was under threat of being dropped, but Monza is a welcome staple in changing times for Formula One, as it's a great circuit with a long and illustrious history.

Some circuits have soul, others have yet to acquire it and some never will. Monza has it in spades, though, as is only fitting for a circuit that has excited and enthralled fans since 1922 and one that is the only one to have hosted a grand prix every year since the formation of the modern era in 1950. Glance at the defunct banked sections that were used last in 1961 and which now lie in a state of disrepair in the woods next to the paddock, and that history is obvious. As is the challenge that the circuit used to provide in the days before its flat-out blasts were interrupted by chicanes. This is, after all, the circuit that held the record for hosting the fastest grand prix of all time, in 1971, when not only was Peter Gethin the first of five cars across the line covered by 0.61s but also did so

at an average speed of more than 150mph. That was finally bettered in 2003, when Michael Schumacher's winning average was 3mph faster; something that becomes even more special when you consider the three chicanes that weren't there in Gethin's day slowed his lap.

In essence, Monza is a high-speed circuit through a wooded setting with a few chicanes slowing its flow. It's more than that, though, especially for Italian fans, who come in their tens of thousands to watch their beloved Ferraris race. Actually, that's not true: they turn up to watch them win. Nothing else will do, as was shown in Ferrari's weaker years when the *tifosi* would leave before the race was over if the red cars had retired. Partisan they may be, but they display a passion that is not seen anywhere else.

INSIDE TRACK

ITALIAN GRAND PRIX

Date:	**4 September**
Circuit length:	**3.600 miles/5.793km**
Number of laps:	**53**
Lap record:	**R Barrichello (Ferrari), 1m21.046s, 159.899mph/257.321kph, 2004**
Telephone:	**00 39 39 24821**
Website:	**www.monzanet.it**

PREVIOUS WINNERS

1995	**Johnny Herbert**	BENETTON
1996	**Michael Schumacher**	FERRARI
1997	**David Coulthard**	McLAREN
1998	**Michael Schumacher**	FERRARI
1999	**Heinz-Harald Frentzen**	JORDAN
2000	**Michael Schumacher**	FERRARI
2001	**Juan Pablo Montoya**	WILLIAMS
2002	**Rubens Barrichello**	FERRARI
2003	**Michael Schumacher**	FERRARI
2004	**Rubens Barrichello**	FERRARI

In the woods: Monza is built in a royal park on the northern outskirts of the town of the same name. This is located just ten miles north-west of Milan.

Shopping mecca: Head for the infield, just beyond the end of the pits, for one of the best shopping arcades at any grand prix, with wonderful shops for books, models, posters and racewear.

Let the train take the strain: The easiest way to reach the circuit is not by car, as traffic can be horrendous, but by train, travelling to Biassono station and then walking in via the first Lesmo corner.

Drivers at work: The Lesmos provide the biggest test, especially the second one, taken in third, trying not to run too wide over the kerbs, before the long, kinked run down to the Ascari chicane.

Where to watch: The first chicane, especially as the drivers pour into there at least two abreast on the opening lap.

The quickest away around Monza is over the kerbs, as demonstrated by Ulsterman Eddie Irvine in 2002

SPA-FRANCORCHAMPS

 Spa-Francorchamps vies with Suzuka for the title of best racing circuit in the world. However, its setting is far more dramatic and this makes it a must-visit location for F1 fans.

The safety car leads Raikkonen, Schumacher and Pizzonia through the new Bus Stop in last year's race

INSIDE TRACK

BELGIAN GRAND PRIX

Date:	**11 September**
Circuit length:	**4.333 miles/6.973km**
Number of laps:	**44**
Lap record:	**K Raikkonen (McLaren), 1m45.108s, 148.407mph/238.827kph, 2004**
Telephone:	**00 32 8727 5138**
Website:	**www.spa-francorchamps.be**

PREVIOUS WINNERS

1994	**Damon Hill** WILLIAMS
1995	**Michael Schumacher** BENETTON
1996	**Michael Schumacher** FERRARI
1997	**Michael Schumacher** FERRARI
1998	**Damon Hill** JORDAN
1999	**David Coulthard** McLAREN
2000	**Mika Hakkinen** McLAREN
2001	**Michael Schumacher** FERRARI
2002	**Michael Schumacher** FERRARI
2004	**Michael Schumacher** FERRARI

Handy from England: Located 35 miles south-east of Liege, Spa-Francorchamps is little more than three hours from Calais. Stay in Spa, Malmedy or Stavelot.

Slice of the past: The town of Stavelot has an excellent circuit museum.

Chips with everything: No visit to Belgium is complete without trying a portion of chips with mayonnaise. For hand-made chocolates, head for Spa.

Drivers at work: Eau Rouge gets the drivers' heart rate going, with its dipping entry and soaring exit, out of which Mark Webber got it wrong last year and tipped Takuma Sato sideways in front of the pack.

Where to watch: Les Combes at the end of the long climb from Eau Rouge, where drivers burst out of the slipstream of the car in front to try and outbrake them into the 90-degree right. La Source is also full of fun on the opening lap.

The Belgian Grand Prix was dropped for 2003 and how everyone missed it: the drivers were deprived of one of their ultimate tests of skill, the fans were denied the chance to watch them really work for their living and the team meteorologists lost their opportunity to show that they can predict the weather in a region where sunshine can turn into rain in a matter of minutes, and often does...

The plus points of this rolling stretch of blacktop in its stunning forest setting high in the Ardennes are almost too numerous to cover here, but there are minus points too - namely a paddock that is cramped for the team transporters although spacious for their motorhomes, as well as security staff who frequently overstep the mark and move photographers from their rightful place just before the start of the race.

The sheer majesty of corners such as Eau Rouge, Pouhon and Blanchimont is unrivalled, though, all of which demand the ultimate in concentration. Unusually for a tough circuit, it is also possible to overtake here, although the reshaping of the left-right, right-left Bus Stop for last year made matters worse rather than better on this count.

For all the inevitable changes, the character of the original circuit remains, although its safety is a world ahead now that barriers line the track rather than sturdy trees... If a driver got it wrong over the crest of Les Combes, into which the track used to feed for a flat-out blast, the outcome was a visit to the next valley - a stark illustration of the bravery of drivers until 1970, after which the race was dropped from the World Championship because it was considered too dangerous. This is highlighted by the fact that Pedro Rodriguez's race-winning average speed that year was 149.9mph...

INTERLAGOS

 Interlagos is a bear pit, a great stretch of bucking and twisting tarmac made all the more memorable by the sheer passion and vigour of the partisan Brazilian crowd.

Ralf Schumacher leads the Renault duo up the circuit's undulating start/finish straight back in 2002

Formula One excites South American sports fans, as it should since the continent has produced multiple world champions Juan Manuel Fangio, Emerson Fittipaldi, Nelson Piquet and Ayrton Senna. For now, Argentina is side-lined, with no race of its own, making the Brazilian Grand Prix all the more important as it's racing's most prestigious category's only visit to the continent.

The Interlagos circuit, although constantly tweaked, remains an anachronism, lagging far behind all other permanent circuits visited by Formula One in terms of its pit and paddock facilities. For now, though, Formula One needs to be at Interlagos as it needs to have a foothold in South America. In fact, all racing fans will be delighted to know that Interlagos' contract to host the grand prix has been extended up to and including 2009.

Situated outside the city boundaries when it opened in 1940, Interlagos has long since been subsumed into the city, but the grassy expanses between the sweeping lower sections of the circuit and undeveloped hills in the distance suggest a rural setting. What gives the track its character, though, is the way it dips, twists and climbs again, keeping the drivers on their toes through the likes of the Descida do Sul esses, Ferradura and Mergulho. Best of all, almost every metre of track can be seen from most of the grandstands that line the top of the hill, as the track runs through a natural amphitheatre. Combine that with the colourful ebullience of the crowd and you have a race worth visiting.

SUZUKA

It may only have been part of the show since 1987, but Suzuka already feels like one of the old guard, a bastion of traditional values in a changing world. Undoubtedly one of the best circuits.

The mark of a circuit that will be enjoyed by drivers is one that has a flow to it rather than the stop-start nature of all too many circuits. The key is to test the driver to the full, to throw in several really difficult corners, too, so that any driver who is on the wrong exit line from one corner will struggle to get onto the right entry line for the following turn. Suzuka is one such track, where a driver's lack of ability is made clear by too many seconds on the stopwatch.

The home of the Japanese Grand Prix is more a test of man than of machine, which is how it should be. Its double-apex opening corner is a clear hint of what is to follow, being downhill on entry and uphill on exit and narrow throughout. That's nothing compared to what follows, with the uphill 'S curves' one of the trickiest stretches of tarmac used in Formula

One. It may not come as much of a surprise, but Michael Schumacher is peerless through here.

Crossover is unique, as it's the only place where a circuit feeds under another section of the same lap, as the track feeds out into the wooded 'country' section of the circuit. Spoon Curve marks the far end of the circuit and it's also the highest point before the charge back down to the pit straight, with the famed 130R left-hander – slightly less scary nowadays, but still a 160mph corner.

Designed by the man responsible for Zandvoort, John Hugenholtz, at the behest of Honda, Suzuka opened in 1963, but only landed a grand prix in 1987. Before that, the honour of hosting the Japanese Grand Prix, which has only been awarded twice before, fell both times to the Fuji Speedway in the mid-1970s.

INSIDE TRACK

JAPANESE GRAND PRIX

Date:	9 October
Circuit length:	3.608 miles/5.806km
Number of laps:	53
Lap record:	R Barrichello (Ferrari), 1m32.730s, 139.998mph/225.294kph, 2004
Telephone:	00 81 593 783620
Website:	www.SuzukaCircuit.co.jp

PREVIOUS WINNERS

1995	Michael Schumacher	BENETTON
1996	Damon Hill	WILLIAMS
1997	Michael Schumacher	FERRARI
1998	Mika Hakkinen	McLAREN
1999	Mika Hakkinen	McLAREN
2000	Michael Schumacher	FERRARI
2001	Michael Schumacher	FERRARI
2002	Michael Schumacher	FERRARI
2003	Rubens Barrichello	FERRARI
2004	Michael Schumacher	FERRARI

You can see the sea: Suzuka is located 50km south-west of Nagoya and 150km east of Osaka, just inland from the sea.

It's a rollercoaster: The circuit is part of a huge funfair complex.

Sting in the tail: The Japanese Grand Prix has always been held late in the season, moving from the penultimate slot to the final one in 1996, taking over from Australia. It was moved ahead of the European GP in 1997 and Malaysia in 2000, regained the honour in 2001 before losing it again to Brazil last year.

Drivers at work: Spoon Curve, as it goes right on entry then it's left, left and left some more, going over a brow and tightening. Exit speed is crucial as it leads onto Suzuka's longest straight.

Where to watch: Casio Triangle, that second gear left-right flick over a crest where so many drivers clatter into others or simply bounce off the kerbs.

Rubens Barrichello powers through the only crossover in Formula One en route to victory in 2003

SHANGHAI

Shanghai International Circuit took F1 on to a new plain, at a stroke making all other venues look outdated. It showed what massive government backing of $240m could achieve.

INSIDE TRACK

CHINESE GRAND PRIX

Date:	**16 October**
Circuit length:	**3.390 miles/5.450km**
Number of laps:	**57**
Lap record:	**M Schumacher (Ferrari), 1m32.238s, 132.202mph/212.749kph, 2004**
Telephone:	**00 86 2162520000**
Website:	**www.f1china.com.cn**

PREVIOUS WINNERS

2004	**Rubens Barrichello** FERRARI

A flying start: A race day crowd of 150,000 for your maiden grand prix is impressive by any standards. But with a population of close on 1.3 billion people, there's quite a pond to fish from when Formula One visits China.

A little pricey: With grandstand tickets costing $170 per throw, they were beyond the pockets of all but the wealthiest of the country's populace.

Who will be first?: The race is on to be the first Chinese driver into Formula One, with Williams setting the pace by giving Dutch-born Formula Three racer Ho-Pin Tung a test in one of its cars and emblazoning his face over their posters around the track. McLaren is backing native-born 'Franky' Cheng Confu.

Tobacco happy: One of the attractions of racing in China is that there are no restrictions on tobacco advertising, and there's a massive population of smokers...

Drivers at work: The first corner is a really tricky piece of Tarmac that goes on and on to the right, tightening its arc as it goes before spitting the driver out directly into a tight left.

Where to watch: At the penultimate corner where drivers have a go under braking, but sometimes get it wrong as David Coulthard did when he rammed Ralf Schumacher.

Rubens Barrichello leads into the first corner at the inaugural Chinese Grand Prix at the distinctive track

Formula One will never be the same again as the inaugural visit to Shanghai International Circuit upped the ante to a new level. The massive grandstands with two balcony storeys above the start/finish straight are distinctive, as are the round-topped 'umbrellas' above the grandstands before the final corner. However, although the track itself is in the shape of the Chinese shang symbol, little else made it obvious that this was a sporting venue in China, the gravel traps and advertising banners being the same as at any other Formula One venue. However, the steel and glass team offices and sponsors' lodges sent one reeling.

This was architecture of the highest order and light years ahead of the motorhomes of old. The racing surface also came in for praise both from the drivers and the TV audiences worldwide, as it was wide enough to allow overtaking, something that was aided by heavy braking into tight corners after long straights, such as the one into the hairpin that's the penultimate corner. Even Michael Schumacher thought that some of the corners were tricky as their entries were blind, with others finding the ever-tightening first corner sequence quite a challenge.

What the Chinese made of their first grand prix remains to be seen, but they turned out in their tens of thousands and really had a lot of action to turn them into the sort of fans who will dial in to every grand prix in 2005, which is just what the sponsors will be hoping for, especially the motor manufacturers who have an eye on the world's fastest-growing automotive market.

Overview of the pit
straight at Shanghai:
the circuit took just 18
months to build and holds
up to 200,000 spectators

REVIEW OF THE 2004 SEASON

Michael Schumacher started last season as a six-time world champion and ended it with seven titles to his name. Almost needless to say, Ferrari blitzed the opposition who could only challenge them occasionally, with Schumacher's team-mate Barrichello the best of the rest.

After pushing Michael Schumacher so close in 2003, Kimi Raikkonen had high hopes for 2004, especially as it was felt that McLaren wouldn't produce two duff cars in a row after the disappointment of its stillborn MP4-18. Williams, too, felt that its "walrus nose" FW26 would be the tool to crack Ferrari's nut. Both were put straight at the opening round of the year as Ferrari turned up in Melbourne and dominated. The rest were also-rans.

Michael Schumacher started on a roll and only a collision in the tunnel at Monaco with Juan Pablo Montoya stopped his run at five straight wins. That he bounced back to win the next seven races only served to deflate the others and, unfortunately, to turn some of the crowds away. At least in 2003, Raikkonen and Montoya had stayed with him in the race for points. This time, he was out on his own. In fact, Michael wrapped up the title in the 14th of the 18 rounds, the Belgian Grand Prix. All was not darkness and gloom for his rivals, though, as he was beaten fair and square that day. The winner was Raikkonen and McLaren's renaissance with its second-generation MP4-19 (the MP4-19B) that had been introduced mid-season almost brought tears of joy to the eyes of McLaren boss Ron Dennis.

Amazingly, Michael then endured two races in which he was, at best, second-best. His performance in Italy, where he spun on the opening lap and had to fight his way back through to second when the Ferraris came good as the conditions changed, was mixed. It was even patchier in China, with a clash another spin and 12th place. But his predominance in the penultimate race in Japan showed that he'd rediscovered his focus. Team-mate Rubens Barrichello was

the man of the moment at Imola and Shanghai, gaining reward for some strong drives early in the year when he could, and perhaps should, have toppled the great man.

Even the *tifosi* will have acknowledged, though, that Formula One needs a battle for the lead, preferably between drivers from different teams. In fact, even better, between drivers from many different teams, but the Ferrari-Bridgestone combination in 2004 was simply too much for any of the other nine teams, with the Japanese tyre supplier raising its game as it addressed rival Michelin's strong points. It must be said, too, that they were flattered by cooler-than-expected weather in the first three races, but their continued push for excellence was apparent right to the final round.

BAR scored a mere 26 points as they ranked fifth overall in 2003. That was easily

their best season until then, yet it was nothing compared to their 2004 campaign in which an excellent Geoff Willis-designed chassis and considerably stronger engines from Honda converted them into the main thorn in Ferrari's side. Jenson Button did everything but win as he made ten visits to the podium over the course of the season. Takuma Sato backed him up with a third-place finish at the US GP. Renault ought to have been the best of the rest, but the wheels came off their challenge in the final third of the season and they never built on Jarno Trulli's immaculate win at Monaco. In fact, they'd fired him before the year was out and Alonso was forced to retire too often, too.

Williams and McLaren both flattered to deceive, although McLaren made clear progress after its MP4-19 was superseded at the French GP and Williams found its feet in

the final flyaways, scoring an excellent win in that final race in Brazil; both teams will have been chastened by their overall form.

Sauber, with its excellent Petronas-badged Ferrari engines and useful pedallers in Giancarlo Fisichella and Felipe Massa, scrapped for the final points, helped by the fact that points are allotted all the way down to eighth place, and were secure in sixth place ahead of four teams – Jaguar, Toyota, Jordan and Minardi – for whom little goes right. Three of these have the excuse of limited budgets, while Toyota will have to start delivering in 2005 or more heads will roll. The German-based Japanese manufacturer's team peaked with Olivier Panis' fifth place in the US GP. For the other three, though, survival was the main thing on their mind and it was Jaguar that lost out when parent company Ford's bean-counters called time.

AUSTRALIAN GP

They said that Ferrari had built too conservative a car to stay in front. They were wrong, though, as Michael Schumacher started from pole and led every lap of the race to lay down a marker for the 17 races to follow.

Whatever the relative form in close-season testing, all the team chiefs knew that they would only discover who had come up with the goods when they hit the track for the opening race of the season. BAR had high hopes, as did Williams, while McLaren were less optimistic, but no one knew quite where Ferrari would stand. Then their worst fears were realised. Ferrari might have produced a car that looked unexciting in specification but, by golly, it was every bit as competitive as its predecessor. Michael Schumacher and Rubens Barrichello locked out the front row of the grid, half a second clear of Juan Pablo Montoya's Williams. And, unlike previous years, they did so with their new car, rather than delaying its debut until the third or fourth race of the season as had been their habit.

Strangely, despite having two-plane rear wings in place of the previous three-plane wings, and with engines that were built to last the entire meeting rather than just through qualifying, all the cars were notably faster than their 2003 antecedents, with Michael's pole time fully 2.755s faster than the mark set in 2003. That says an awful lot for the engine-builders at Maranello, who had clearly pulled off the trick of making their engines both more durable and more powerful.

Ferrari's stars were all in alignment as a cool race day dawned. The temperature remained considerably below the seasonal norm - something that benefited the Ferrari's Bridgestone rubber rather than the heat-loving Michelins used by their rivals. And how they made this advantage pay. That Michael and Rubens finished first and second in the race - with Rubens 13.6s behind - was bad enough for their rivals, but what made it all the more crushing was that the next best finisher, Renault's Fernando Alonso, was almost 35s down on Michael after 58 laps of racing and he, in turn, was more than 25s ahead of the fourth-placed finisher, Williams's Ralf Schumacher.

It was worse still for McLaren: they came away with only one point, for David Coulthard's eighth place, in this the season when they had hoped to reassert themselves over Ferrari. What's more, the Scot had been lapped... Still, at least he reached the finish line, unlike team-mate Kimi Raikkonen who had pulled off with engine failure as the season's first retirement after only nine laps. It wasn't as though he lost a good result, either, as he'd been running 11th at the time, one place behind Coulthard, with both struggling in the corners...

While the Ferrari duo didn't put a foot wrong, the same couldn't be said of Montoya, who tried to brave it out with Alonso's fast-starting Renault into the first corner and ran wide, falling to seventh place, a position from which he could only recover to fifth by the chequered flag.

There were three new boys in the race, with Jaguar's Christian Klien best-placed at the finish in 11th, three places ahead of Jordan's Giorgio Pantano, while Gianmaria Bruni made a flying start in his Minardi, only to spend 17 minutes in the pits while a misfire was sorted.

Michael Schumacher salutes the Ferrari pit crew after getting his 2004 campaign off to a winning start

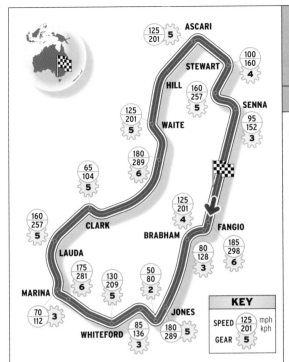

POLE TIME
M Schumacher, 1m24.408s, 140.532mph/226.153kph

WINNER'S AVERAGE SPEED
136.093mph/219.010kph

FASTEST LAP
M Schumacher, 1m24.125s, 141.016mph/226.933kph

LAP LEADERS
M Schumacher, 1–58

 MELBOURNE ROUND 1

Date **7 March 2004** Laps **58** Distance **191.11 miles/307.55km**
Weather **Warm, dry and overcast**

RACE RESULT

Position	Driver	Team	Result	Stops	Qualifying Time	Grid
1	Michael Schumacher	Ferrari	1h24m15.757s	3	1m24.408s	1
2	Rubens Barrichello	Ferrari	1h24m29.362s	3	1m24.482s	2
3	Fernando Alonso	Renault	1h24m50.430s	3	1m25.699s	5
4	Ralf Schumacher	Williams	1h25m16.180s	3	1m25.925s	8
5	Juan Pablo Montoya	Williams	1h25m24.293s	3	1m24.998s	3
6	Jenson Button	BAR	1h25m26.355s	3	1m24.998s	4
7	Jarno Trulli	Renault	57 laps	3	1m26.290s	9
8	David Coulthard	McLaren	57 laps	2	1m27.294s	12
9	Takuma Sato	BAR	57 laps	3	1m25.851s	7
10	Giancarlo Fisichella	Sauber	57 laps	3	1m27.845s	14
11	Christian Klien	Jaguar	56 laps	2	No time	19
12	Cristiano da Matta	Toyota	56 laps	3	1m27.823s	13
13	Olivier Panis	Toyota	56 laps	2	No time	18
14	Giorgio Pantano	Jordan	55 laps	2	1m30.140s	16
R	Felipe Massa	Sauber	44 laps/engine	2	1m27.065s	11
R	Nick Heidfeld	Jordan	43 laps/clutch	3	1m28.178s	15
NC	Gianmaria Bruni	Minardi	43 laps	3	No time	20
R	Mark Webber	Jaguar	29 laps/transmission	2	1m25.805s	6
R	Zsolt Baumgartner	Minardi	13 laps/electronics	1	1m30.681s	17
R	Kimi Raikkonen	McLaren	9 laps/engine	0	1m26.297s	10

TALKING POINT: THE NEW QUALIFYING FORMAT

The quest to make Formula One more exciting by re-jigging the rules fell at the first hurdle with the revised qualifying format. The practicalities of running the session over 90 minutes, with the drivers' first run times determining the order in which they go out for their second run, with the fastest going last, was considered a flop. There was too little excitement as the cars lapped one by one. Solutions for changing it were immediately under discussion. It made many hanker after the free-for-all sessions when drivers were each allowed 12 laps.

Klien crumbles under the pressure of qualifying

MALAYSIAN GP

Reigning champion Michael Schumacher made it two in a row for Ferrari, but Williams ace Juan Pablo Montoya chased him every inch of the way. However, lap after lap, Michael was always in complete control of the race and that was what worried his rivals the most: they rapidly got the feeling he was merely toying with them.

Rubens Barrichello leads Juan Pablo Montoya on the first lap, just before the Ferrari driver slid wide

Barrichello who had slotted in behind him. The reds were in control, as they had been in the opening round in Australia. A light shower five minutes before the start of the race, however, had put a different complexion on proceedings and the man on the move, revelling in the slippery conditions, was Juan Pablo Montoya. The Colombian passed the Brazilian when he ran wide early on the second lap and closed in on the leader. The rain then eased off just as he got on to the red car's tail. He had a look at making a move on the third lap, but waited and never found himself in a position to have another go, when Michael edged clear as the track dried. Stopping three laps later than Michael for fuel and new tyres pushed Montoya into the lead, but after lap 12, never again, even though the first part of his second and third stints would see him close up again before his rubber started to wear. Emerging in traffic took the edge off his fourth stint and he had reason to be as unhappy on the podium as Michael looked jubilant.

Happiest of all on the podium, though, was Jenson Button, who finally achieved the top-three finish that had been snatched away from him at this very track on the final lap of the race in 2002. This really marked BAR's ascendancy, and the fact that he was able to win a straight fight with Barrichello was clear evidence of the team's progress.

Renault showed good speed at Sepang, but they were erratic as Alonso fell off in qualifying and had to start from the rear of the grid. Jarno Trulli made one of Renault's regular scorching getaways, but he clipped Button at the first corner and then lost ground when running wide. Thereafter, he settled down to finish fifth.

Once again the McLarens were also-rans, with Coulthard sixth and Raikkonen again disappointed by an engine failure. And this from a less-than-competitive Mercedes engine...

If Rubens Barrichello somehow still harboured any notions that he was equal number one at Ferrari then he was disabused of these when he was sent back to Europe after the Australian GP to undertake testing of the latest Bridgestone tyres while Michael Schumacher relaxed on the beach in Malaysia. The Japanese tyre manu-facturer was anxious to improve its tyres' hot-weather form, an area in which the Michelins have long been superior. His work paid dividends, but only for Michael, as when it came to the cut-off time of 9am on the Saturday the

team elected to send their drivers out on different compounds, with Rubens on the harder and more stable one and Michael on the trickier, but potentially faster, softer one. With the luck of the devil, Michael came up trumps yet again when the temperature, normally scalding in Malaysia, plummeted on race day. Michelin's gun was spiked.

Michael had qualified on pole, but was faced with a new challenger on the outside of the front row, Mark Webber (see Talking Point). By the first corner, however, it was team-mate

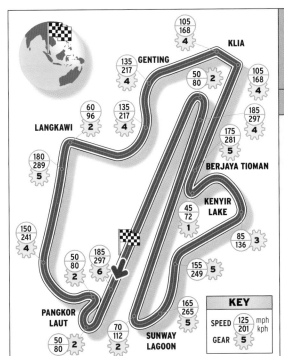

105 / 168 / 4
KLIA

GENTING
135 / 217 / 4
50 / 80 / 2
105 / 168 / 4

60 / 96 / 2
135 / 217 / 4
185 / 297 / 4

LANGKAWI

175 / 281 / 5

180 / 289 / 5

BERJAYA TIOMAN

KENYIR LAKE
45 / 72 / 1

85 / 136 / 3

150 / 241 / 4
50 / 80 / 2
185 / 297 / 6
155 / 249 / 5

165 / 265 / 5

PANGKOR LAUT

70 / 112 / 2
SUNWAY LAGOON

50 / 80 / 2

KEY

| SPEED | 125 / 201 | mph / kph |
| GEAR | 5 | |

POLE TIME

M Schumacher, 1m33.074s, 133.210mph/214.371kph

WINNER'S AVERAGE SPEED

126.998mph/204.374kph

FASTEST LAP

Montoya, 1m34.223s, 131.595mph/211.772kph

LAP LEADERS

M Schumacher, 1-9, 13-26, 28-56; Montoya, 10-12; Barrichello, 27

 SEPANG ROUND 2

Date **21 March 2004** Laps **56** Distance **192.864 miles/310.37km**
Weather **Warm, dry and bright**

RACE RESULT

Position	Driver	Team	Result	Stops	Qualifying Time	Grid
1	**Michael Schumacher**	Ferrari	1h31m07.490s	3	1m33.074s	1
2	**Juan Pablo Montoya**	Williams	1h31m12.512s	3	1m34.054s	4
3	**Jenson Button**	BAR	1h31m19.058s	3	1m34.221s	6
4	**Rubens Barrichello**	Ferrari	1h31m21.106s	3	1m33.756s	3
5	**Jarno Trulli**	Renault	1h31m44.850s	3	1m34.413s	8
6	**David Coulthard**	McLaren	1h32m00.588s	3	1m34.602s	9
7	**Fernando Alonso**	Renault	1h32m15.367s	2	No time	19
8	**Felipe Massa**	Sauber	55 laps	3	1m35.039s	11
9	**Cristiano da Matta**	Toyota	55 laps	3	1m34.917s	10
10	**Christian Klien**	Jaguar	55 laps	3	1m35.158s	13
11	**Giancarlo Fisichella**	Sauber	55 laps	3	1m35.061s	12
12	**Olivier Panis**	Toyota	55 laps	5	1m35.617s	14
13	**Giorgio Pantano**	Jordan	54 laps	2	1m39.902s	18
14	**Gianmaria Bruni**	Minardi	53 laps	3	1m38.577s	16
15	**Takuma Sato**	BAR	52 laps/engine	2	No time	20
16	**Zsolt Baumgartner**	Minardi	52 laps	3	1m39.272s	17
R	**Kimi Raikkonen**	McLaren	40 laps/engine	3	1m34.602s	9
R	**Nick Heidfeld**	Jordan	34 laps/gearbox	4	1m36.569s	15
R	**Ralf Schumacher**	Williams	27 laps/engine	1	1m34.235s	7
R	**Mark Webber**	Jaguar	23 laps/spun off	2	1m33.715s	2

TALKING POINT: JAGUAR'S FALSE DAWN

Jaguar had every reason to smile at Sepang as Mark Webber had given them their best-ever grid position after qualifying second. This was on merit, too, and not the result of going out with a light fuel load. Sadly, both Mark and team-mate Christian Klien were blighted at the start when the anti-stall mechanism lost its mind. In a flash, Mark fell from second to a middle-of-the-grid position. An assault from Ralf Schumacher left him with a puncture. He then received a stop-go penalty for speeding in the pits, before later spinning off with damaged handling.

Moments after this, Webber's Jaguar was left standing

BAHRAIN GP

Going into uncharted territory clearly held no mysteries for Ferrari as their drivers Michael Schumacher and Rubens Barrichello romped home on Formula One's first visit to the Gulf States. Much of the talk afterwards was of the Bahraini hosts and the magnificent job they had done with their new no-expense-spared circuit.

As much as the 2003 World Championship had been competitive, with Ferrari being challenged hard by both Williams and McLaren and, to a lesser extent, by Renault, it was clear by as early as the third round of the 2004 season that the Italian team was again well out front and in a class of its own.

If success on Sunday means sales on Monday, then Ferrari will have done extremely well in cash-rich Bahrain and the Manama rush hour may well be speckled with more cars carrying a prancing horse badge on their noses after this one-two.

Qualifying resulted in another all-Ferrari front row, but Williams' Juan Pablo Montoya wasn't far off Barrichello's pace. However, he had gambled everything on getting onto the front row by opting to run a soft-tyre compound. As this would also have to be his chosen rubber the following day, he was never likely to run as close in the race. And so it proved, but it was an obstructive gearbox that did the most damage to his chances, dropping him from third to a lapped 13th in the closing ten laps.

So, with Montoya slipping backwards, Button thanked his lucky stars and made it two podium positions on the trot. It must be pointed out, though, that, pleased as he was, Jenson was fully aware that he had crossed the finish line almost half a minute behind the reigning world champion. Part of the reason for this huge gap is that the weather again played into Ferrari's hands and a drop of ten degrees on race day – even with rain that's very rare in Bahrain – helped them on their Bridgestone tyres.

The Ferraris had one moment of concern, when Michael locked up into the first corner and Barrichello had to lift off in order to avoid him, allowing Montoya and friends to get closer to him than he would have liked.

Jarno Trulli made another cracking start and demoted Button on the run to the first corner, but the Englishman got into his stride as the race advanced and was able to demote the Italian, to a fourth-place finish that was comfortably clear of Button's team-mate, Takuma Sato. Ralf Schumacher only had himself to blame after thumping Sato's BAR in a move that earned him both a reprimand and a check-up in the pits and left him in an eventual seventh place.

After qualifying so well at Sepang, Mark Webber was back in 14th on the grid, two places behind team-mate Christian Klien. He did have some excitement, though, when Fernando Alonso was trying to pass him and he thought it was Trulli coming up to lap him and sought clarification from his pitcrew. When it was confirmed that it was Alonso and the move was for position, he moved into the Spaniard's path, leading to a dicey moment. Alonso had the last laugh, though, by finishing sixth.

The most worrying matter for the nine teams chasing Ferrari was that this stop-start track wasn't one that was supposed to have suited the Italian cars...

Michael Schumacher leads into the first corner as Rubens Barrichello tucks in to his regular supporting role

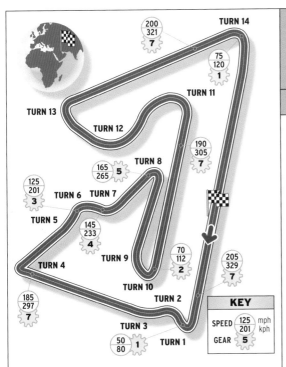

TURN 14
TURN 11
TURN 13
TURN 12
TURN 8
TURN 6 **TURN 7**
TURN 5
TURN 4
TURN 9
TURN 10
TURN 2
TURN 3
TURN 1

KEY		
SPEED	125 / 201	mph / kph
GEAR	5	

POLE TIME

M Schumacher, 1m30.139s, 135.750mph/218.459kph

WINNER'S AVERAGE SPEED

129.580mph/208.529kph

FASTEST LAP

M Schumacher, 1m30.252s, 134.260mph/216.061kph

LAP LEADERS

M Schumacher, 1-9, 12-24, 28-41, 44-57; Barrichello, 10, 25-27, 42-43

 SAKHIR ROUND 3

Date **4 April 2004** Laps **57** Distance **191.86 miles/308.76km**
Weather **Warm, dry and bright**

RACE RESULT

Position	Driver	Team	Result	Stops	Qualifying Time	Grid
1	Michael Schumacher	Ferrari	1h28m34.875s	3	1m30.139s	1
2	Rubens Barrichello	Ferrari	1h28m36.242s	3	1m30.530s	2
3	Jenson Button	BAR	1h29m01.562s	3	1m30.856s	6
4	Jarno Trulli	Renault	1h29m07.089s	3	1m30.971s	7
5	Takuma Sato	BAR	1h29m27.335s	3	1m30.827s	5
6	Fernando Alonso	Renault	1h29m28.031s	3	1m34.130s	17
7	Ralf Schumacher	Williams	1h29m33.030s	3	1m30.633s	4
8	Mark Webber	Jaguar	56 laps	3	1m32.625s	14
9	Olivier Panis	Toyota	56 laps	3	1m31.686s	8
10	Cristiano da Matta	Toyota	56 laps	3	1m31.717s	9
11	Giancarlo Fisichella	Sauber	56 laps	3	1m31.731s	11
12	Felipe Massa	Sauber	56 laps	3	1m32.625s	13
13	Juan Pablo Montoya	Williams	56 laps	3	1m30.581s	3
14	Christian Klien	Jaguar	56 laps	3	1m32.332s	12
15	Nick Heidfeld	Jordan	56 laps	2	1m33.506s	15
16	Giorgio Pantano	Jordan	55 laps	3	1m34.105s	16
17	Gianmaria Bruni	Minardi	52 laps	2	1m34.584s	18
R	David Coulthard	McLaren	50 laps/hydraulics	4	1m31.719s	10
R	Zsolt Baumgartner	Minardi	44 laps/engine	3	1m35.787s	19
R	Kimi Raikkonen	McLaren	7 laps/engine	0	No time	20

TALKING POINT: ROLLING STONES

It's not every year that F1 tries a new circuit. Then, like buses, two come along at the same time. The Bahrain International Circuit at Sakhir was a hit. Having won its race against time to be ready for its opening, the new track – on the site of a former camel farm – was well received. If there was any criticism, it was that the application of a layer of glue to any sandy areas near the track failed to work as stones were kicked up whenever a driver ran wide, leading to a host of punctures. A surface such as Astroturf has been suggested for 2005.

Rubens Barrichello flies by on Bahrain's desert track

SAN MARINO GP

BAR's upward curve continued at Imola, but Jenson Button's pole position and subsequent early lead was only a distraction, as Michael Schumacher took his time before striking to make it four wins on the trot.

BAR's Jenson Button leads the field into the first corner on the opening lap with Michael Schumacher keeping the Williams drivers in his Ferrari's wake

Definitely a contender for the lap of the year, Jenson Button's pole lap was a blinder and his BAR 006's handling was superb. As he threaded it through the final sector of the lap, he was able to use more kerb than any of his rivals, and crossed the line in 1m19.753s. No other driver, not even local hero Michael Schumacher, could break 1m20s, and the 24-year-old Englishman had netted his first pole position. Small wonder the BAR pitcrew exploded with delight. With team-mate Takuma Sato fast enough for seventh, they had really set the cat among the pigeons and were now mixing it comfortably with the likes of Williams and Renault.

Beating the Ferrari team leader in qualifying is one thing, but putting one over him in the race, on the team's home ground, is quite another. So, although Button powered into a clear lead at the start, he was not able to stay ahead. This wasn't to say that Schumacher had it easy. Indeed, it was anything but for the

German over the first half of the opening lap. Juan Pablo Montoya had been quicker away from the start and put the Ferrari under pressure into Villeneuve. This move was countered, but the Colombian wasn't defeated and tried again at the next corner, the Tosa hairpin. He went for the outside and Schumacher simply made sure that he drove out to the edge of the track on the exit, forcing Montoya onto the grass. A furious Montoya didn't lift, but Schumacher was safe in second and Montoya had to be harsh to hold onto third, putting the other Schumacher, Ralf, his own team-mate, on to the grass on the other side of the circuit.

With all this going on, Button was free to make the most of his Michelins - tyres that get up to optimum temperature sooner than the Bridgestones - and crossed the start-finish line already 2.7s to the good. However, the Ferrari that had won the first three races of the campaign then started to hit its pace and the

six-time world champion was on the Englishman's tail by the time that he pitted at the end of nine laps. Two flying laps later, Schumacher came in for the first of his three stops and the job was done as he emerged in front and was never to surrender the lead again, beating Button to the finish by ten seconds. It was still the Englishman's best result, though.

Montoya was a further 12 seconds adrift, just ahead of Fernando Alonso, who had clashed with Ralf Schumacher, spinning him down to seventh with 12 laps to go. Jarno Trulli finished fifth in the second Renault, just ahead of Rubens Barrichello, who failed in a last-lap dive for position.

McLaren's woes were evident; even though Kimi Raikkonen finally scored his first point, he was lapped in eighth after starting last. David Coulthard was over-ambitious at the start, attempting to make up for qualifying 11th, and had to pit for a new nose and could only make it back to 12th.

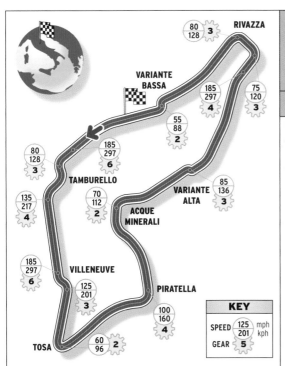

KEY
SPEED	125 / 201	mph / kph
GEAR	5	

POLE TIME
Button, 1m19.753s, 138.307mph/222.573kph

WINNER'S AVERAGE SPEED
131.691mph/211.926kph

FASTEST LAP
M Schumacher, 1m20.411s, 137.175mph/220.752kph

LAP LEADERS
Button, 1-8; M Schumacher, 9-62

IMOLA ROUND 4
Date **25 April 2004** Laps **62** Distance **189.968 miles/305.710km**
Weather **Warm, dry and bright**

RACE RESULT

Position	Driver	Team	Result	Stops	Qualifying Time	Grid
1	**Michael Schumacher**	Ferrari	1h26m19.670s	3	1m20.011s	2
2	**Jenson Button**	BAR	1h26m29.372s	3	1m19.753s	1
3	**Juan Pablo Montoya**	Williams	1h26m41.287s	3	1m20.212s	3
4	**Fernando Alonso**	Renault	1h26m43.324s	3	1m20.895s	6
5	**Jarno Trulli**	Renault	1h26m55.886s	3	1m21.034s	9
6	**Rubens Barrichello**	Ferrari	1h26m56.353s	3	1m20.451s	4
7	**Ralf Schumacher**	Williams	1h27m15.400s	3	1m20.538s	5
8	**Kimi Raikkonen**	McLaren	61 laps	2	No time	20
9	**Giancarlo Fisichella**	Sauber	61 laps	2	No time	19
10	**Felipe Massa**	Sauber	61 laps	3	1m21.532s	12
11	**Olivier Panis**	Toyota	61 laps	3	1m21.558s	13
12	**David Coulthard**	McLaren	61 laps	2	1m21.091s	11
13	**Mark Webber**	Jaguar	61 laps	3	1m20.921s	8
14	**Christian Klien**	Jaguar	60 lap	3	1m21.949s	14
15	**Zsolt Baumgartner**	Minardi	58 laps	3	1m46.299s	18
16	**Takuma Sato**	BAR	56 laps/engine	3	1m20.913s	7
R	**Nick Heidfeld**	Jordan	48 laps/transmission	3	1m23.488s	16
R	**Cristiano da Matta**	Toyota	32 laps/accident	3	1m21.087s	10
R	**Gianmaria Bruni**	Minardi	22 laps/brakes	3	1m26.899s	17
R	**Giorgio Pantano**	Jordan	6 laps/hydraulics	0	1m23.352s	15

TALKING POINT: ONE FOR THE ROAD

With the World Championship spreading its wings to pastures new beyond the borders of Europe, many F1 regulars were wistfully thinking this may have been Imola's last grand prix before being dropped to admit another country to the circus. Its facilities are outdated, its pitlane and paddock cramped and its access limited, to say nothing of Italy having its own grand prix just down the road at Monza. However, for all its faults, the track that dips and weaves its way through the parkland setting remains one of the best stretches of blacktop visited.

Imola's pits open for visitors before the grand prix

SPANISH GP

Michael Schumacher again found himself second over the opening laps, but the Ferrari supremo continued to dominate as he led home team-mate Rubens Barrichello with Jarno Trulli finishing as best of the rest for Renault.

Watching the Renaults blast away from the grid was one of the best sights of the early races of the season, especially at the Circuit de Catalunya, where Jarno Trulli offered F1 fans the chance to see something other than Michael Schumacher's Ferrari lead the race. Indeed, the Italian was simply mighty as he all but anticipated the start and was fastest away, threading his way past Takuma Sato, Juan Pablo Montoya and Schumacher before the first corner. In an instant, he thwarted all pre-race expectation of a mighty clash between front-row starters Schumacher and Montoya, a pair who had, of course, clashed on the opening lap at the San Marino Grand Prix. Indeed, Montoya was so slow away that he slipped back to fourth behind Sato and was never to be a factor in the race.

Yet, and you always felt as though this would be the case, the German didn't stay behind for long, hitting the front after making his first stop a lap later than Trulli. In fact, the pair ran second and third until lap 17 behind Rubens Barrichello,

who Ferrari had opted to send out on a two-stop strategy as he'd qualified only fifth and would thus have to contend with traffic in the race, unlike Schumacher who could be expected to lead. The Brazilian knuckled down and worked his way up to second place, but was almost tripped up when the Ferrari pitcrew weren't ready for his arrival. Fortunately, the time lost failed to cost him a place, with second place safely his as Trulli simply couldn't keep up and had to settle for third, for only his third-ever visit to the podium.

Schumacher's victory, his 75th, was at one stage far from certain, as his engine started to sound rough during the second of his four race stints. Any expectations that his engine would fail and allow another driver to win, however, came to nothing.

The crowds were massive as the Spanish came to their home race as never before, all hoping to see whether Fernando Alonso could go one better than his 2003 result here of

second place. He couldn't, with his inability to qualify higher than eighth costing him dear as he lost time fighting his way up the order and had to settle for fourth, less than a second behind his team-mate.

Sato matched his best-ever finish by coming home fifth, with Ralf Schumacher disappointing again by placing sixth with fading brakes. Team-mate Juan Pablo Montoya didn't even get that far, after dropping out with the same problem. That still left them better off than McLaren's David Coulthard and Kimi Raikkonen, who both struggled again in qualifying and, although starting well, the cars handled so poorly that they slipped back down the order again to tenth and 11th respectively, leaving both drivers desperate for the arrival of a wholly new chassis mid-season.

Imola hero Jenson Button was the opposite, qualifying only 14th after sliding wide, and then getting bogged down in traffic en route to eighth, even though he set the race's second-fastest lap.

Rubens Barrichello, Michael Schumacher and Jarno Trulli on the podium alongside King Juan Carlos after Michael made it five wins from five at the start of 2004

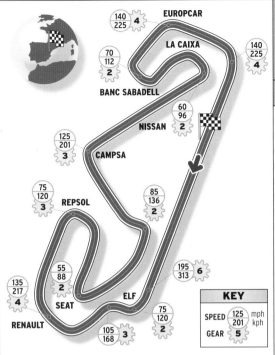

POLE TIME
M Schumacher, 1m15.022s, 137.969mph/222.030kph

WINNER'S AVERAGE SPEED
130.000mph/209.205kph

FASTEST LAP
M Schumacher, 1m17.450s, 133.644mph/215.069kph

LAP LEADERS
Trulli, 1-8; M Schumacher, 9-10, 18-62; Barrichello, 11-17

BARCELONA ROUND 5

Date **9 May 2004** Laps **66** Distance **189.763 miles/305.380km**
Weather **Warm, dry and bright**

RACE RESULT

Position	Driver	Team	Result	Stops	Qualifying Time	Grid
1	Michael Schumacher	Ferrari	1h27m32.841s	3	1m15.022s	1
2	Rubens Barrichello	Ferrari	1h27m46.131s	2	1m16.272s	5
3	Jarno Trulli	Renault	1h28m05.135s	3	1m16.144s	4
4	Fernando Alonso	Renault	1m28m05.793s	3	1m16.422s	8
5	Takuma Sato	BAR	1h28m15.168s	3	1m15.809s	3
6	Ralf Schumacher	Williams	1m28m46.645s	3	1m16.293s	6
7	Giancarlo Fisichella	Sauber	1h28m49.949s	2	1m17.444s	12
8	Jenson Button	BAR	65 laps	3	1m17.575s	14
9	Felipe Massa	Sauber	65 laps	2	1m17.866s	17
10	David Coulthard	McLaren	65 laps	3	1m16.636s	10
11	Kimi Raikkonen	McLaren	65 laps	3	1m17.445s	13
12	Mark Webber	Jaguar	65 laps	3	1m16.514s	9
13	Cristiano da Matta	Toyota	65 laps	3	1m17.038s	11
R	Giorgio Pantano	Jordan	51 laps/hydraulics	3	1m20.607s	19
R	Juan Pablo Montoya	Williams	46 laps/brakes	3	1m15.639s	2
R	Christian Klien	Jaguar	43 laps/throttle	2	1m17.812s	16
R	Olivier Panis	Toyota	33 laps/hydraulics	3	1m16.313s	7
R	Nick Heidfeld	Jordan	33 laps/gearbox	2	1m17.802s	15
R	Gianmaria Bruni	Minardi	31 laps/spun off	2	1m19.817s	18
R	Zsolt Baumgartner	Minardi	17 laps/spun off	1	1m21.470s	20

TALKING POINT: MUSICAL CHAIRS

Williams found its off-track activities of more interest in Spain than its meagre returns in the race: Ralf Schumacher was tipped to follow team-mate Juan Pablo Montoya to pastures new in 2005 and sign for Toyota, thus leaving the team in the unusual position of having to fill both of its seats and triggering a frenzy of gossip. Mark Webber remained the top tip to lead the team, with Jacques Villeneuve joining David Coulthard and Giancarlo Fisichella in the running for the second seat with Indy Racing League pace-setter Scott Dixon as an outsider.

Ralf Schumacher and Juan Pablo Montoya at Catalunya

MONACO GP

Finally, one of Formula One's great enigmas, Jarno Trulli, showed that he could race just as well as he could qualify by holding off Jenson Button in Monte Carlo to score the first of what could be many wins.

Michael Schumacher arrived at Monaco looking to beat Nigel Mansell's record by winning the first six races of the season. However, that script was torn up and thrown away as the German qualified his Ferrari only fourth on this, a circuit where overtaking is so difficult.

The front row was occupied instead by the Renault of Jarno Trulli – who qualified second here in 2000 for Jordan – and BAR's Jenson Button, with Fernando Alonso third-quickest. What impressed everyone was the fact that Trulli's lap was 0.4 seconds faster than Button's, largely due to a brilliant third and final sector. The Italian gave much of the credit to the team's engineers for finding a chassis tweak that transformed the R24's handling. They did this by adding a strut between the monocoque and the engine that offered the drivers the feedback they needed to attack.

Actually, the front of the grid would have looked very different had Ralf Schumacher not suffered engine failure during Thursday practice. This meant that he would have to forfeit ten places on the grid, dropping from second to 12th.

Making the most of pole, Trulli slotted into the lead, with Alonso emphasizing Renault's ability to get its cars off the line to outdrag Button to the first corner. Theirs were not the best start, though, as Takuma Sato blasted the second BAR up from seventh on the grid to sit alongside Button into Ste Devote. Many felt that he had jumped the start, but the sensors failed to detect it if he did. Whatever the case, this was not what Schumacher had wanted as it left the two Renaults leading from the two BARs followed by Kimi Raikkonen's improving McLaren, with Michael sixth.

The race was given its first shake-up when Sato's engine blew on the third lap at Piscine. The smoke was so thick that those behind could see nothing and Giancarlo Fisichella's Sauber ended up inverted after bouncing off David Coulthard's McLaren in the fog. This brought the safety car out.

No looking back: Jarno Trulli of Italy and Renault on his way to victory in last year's grand prix

Button pitted early, followed by Raikkonen, allowing Schumacher to ascend the order, but he was unable to live with the Renaults and only led briefly by pitting after they did; otherwise he was suffering as his Bridgestones were found distinctly wanting around many of the tighter corners.

He was given another chance to close up when the safety car was called out again. This was because Alonso had had an accident in the one place where drivers would least fancy one: in the tunnel, after an incident with Ralf Schumacher (see Talking Point).

It was during this safety-car period that something else happened in the tunnel: Juan Pablo Montoya hit the other Schumacher...

So it came down to a straight race between Trulli, who was driving flawlessly, and Button, who was starting to reel him in. By the end of the race, the gap was just half a second, but Trulli said that he had ignored calls from his pit to speed up and never looked in his mirrors. After a truly unremarkable race, Rubens Barrichello claimed third, helped by Raikkonen's retirement with, you've guessed it, yet another Mercedes engine failure.

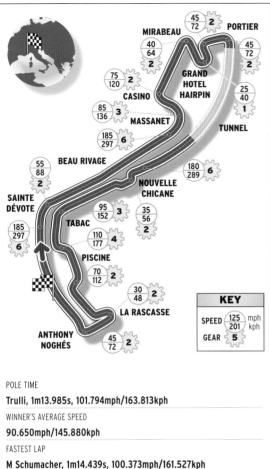

MIRABEAU
45/72 — 2
PORTIER
40/64 — 2
45/72 — 2
GRAND HOTEL HAIRPIN
75/120 — 2
CASINO
25/40 — 1
85/136 — 3
MASSANET
TUNNEL
185/297 — 6
BEAU RIVAGE
55/88 — 2
180/289 — 6
NOUVELLE CHICANE
SAINTE DÉVOTE
95/152 — 3
35/56 — 2
185/297 — 6
TABAC
110/177 — 4
PISCINE
70/112 — 2
30/48 — 2
LA RASCASSE
ANTHONY NOGHÉS
45/72 — 2

KEY

| SPEED | 125 / 201 | mph / kph |
| GEAR | 5 | |

POLE TIME

Trulli, 1m13.985s, 101.794mph/163.813kph

WINNER'S AVERAGE SPEED

90.650mph/145.880kph

FASTEST LAP

M Schumacher, 1m14.439s, 100.373mph/161.527kph

LAP LEADERS

Trulli, 1-23, 26-42, 46-77; Alonso, 24; M Schumacher, 25, 43-45

MONTE CARLO ROUND 6

Date **23 May 2004** Laps **77** Distance **163.176 miles/262.594km**
Weather **Warm, dry and bright**

RACE RESULT

Position	Driver	Team	Result	Stops	Qualifying Time	Grid
1	Jarno Trulli	Renault	1h45m46.601s	2	1m13.985s	1
2	Jenson Button	BAR	1h45m47.098s	2	1m14.396s	2
3	Rubens Barrichello	Ferrari	1h47m02.367s	2	1m14.716s	6
4	Juan Pablo Montoya	Williams	76 laps	2	1m15.039s	9
5	Felipe Massa	Sauber	76 laps	2	1m16.248s	16
6	Cristiano da Matta	Toyota	76 laps	2	1m16.169s	15
7	Nick Heidfeld	Jordan	75 laps	2	1m16.488s	17
8	Olivier Panis	Toyota	74 laps	2	1m15.859s	13
9	Zsolt Baumgartner	Minardi	71 laps	3	1m20.060s	19
10	Ralf Schumacher	Williams	69 laps/gearbox	2	1m14.345s	12
R	Michael Schumacher	Ferrari	45 laps/accident	1	1m14.516s	4
R	Fernando Alonso	Renault	41 laps/accident	1	1m14.408s	3
R	Kimi Raikkonen	McLaren	27 laps/engine	1	1m14.592s	5
R	Gianmaria Bruni	Minardi	15 laps/brakes	2	1m20.115s	20
R	Giorgio Pantano	Jordan	12 laps/hydraulics	1	1m17.443s	18
R	Mark Webber	Jaguar	11 laps/electronics	-	1m15.725s	11
R	Takuma Sato	BAR	2 laps/engine	-	1m14.827s	7
R	Giancarlo Fisichella	Sauber	2 laps/accident	-	1m15.352s	10
R	David Coulthard	McLaren	2 laps/accident	-	1m14.951s	
R	Christian Klien	Jaguar	0 laps/accident	-	1m15.919s	14

TALKING POINT: DARK GOINGS-ON

Monaco's tunnel is as dangerous as it is dark, it's curving and it has only one line through it, as shown when Alonso tried to lap Ralf Schumacher. He claimed that Ralf pulled to the right, then accelerated hard as he went past, forcing his Renault into the barriers. The fact is that Ralf's car was missing gears and thus its acceleration was not predictable. Then, on the final lap of the ensuing safety-car period, Michael Schumacher was warming his brakes by accelerating then slowing, but foolishly did so in the tunnel and Montoya, behind, was caught out, pitching him off...

Fernando Alonso's car lies broken by the chicane

EUROPEAN GP

It was a case of everything returning to normal following the excitement of Monaco, when Renault broke Ferrari's run, as Michael Schumacher resumed his usual supremacy in front of his home fans.

The lap chart said it all: Michael Schumacher had started from pole position, led away at the start, lost the lead by pitting early, then resumed the lead once everyone else had called into the pits and was never headed again. Win number 76 was in the bag and few of them had been easier. On this evidence, any of those who had felt that the Monaco result had produced a ray of hope that Ferrari would not control the season would have left the Nurburgring disappointed.

If you were after an upset, you would have had to look instead towards the Williams hierarchy after team-mates Ralf Schumacher and Juan Pablo Montoya collided on the very first lap. Schumacher then collected Cristiano da Matta's Toyota and headed for the gravel trap. Their races were run, but the Colombian was able to continue after pitting for a new nose. By half distance, he had been lapped, however.

If this clash could have been put down to a "racing accident", then McLaren probably had all

the more reason to be upset as their engine woes continued. Kimi Raikkonen, who had qualified fourth but immediately vaulted into second behind Michael, pulled off with engine failure after just nine laps. What made this failure all the more galling was the fact that, for once, he had been going well. David Coulthard fared no better. He had had to start at the back of the grid as he lost an engine before qualifying, yet he battled his way through to ninth on the opening lap and then on to fourth by running a two-stop strategy. However, he also parked up with a smoking motor and Mercedes chief Jurgen Hubbert was furious that Ilmor had sent a new specification of piston that he said had not been tested fully before being sent to the Nurburgring.

With Williams and McLaren out of the reckoning, Rubens Barrichello found himself challenged by a BAR. It wasn't Jenson Button, though, but Takuma Sato, who had qualified second, been passed by Raikkonen and Fernando Alonso on the opening lap, then got

close enough to make an attempt to pass the Ferrari driver into the tight first corner on lap 46. He was probably too far back, but wanted to make the most of his new tyres while they were at their best and all watching were delighted that he gave it a go, even though they hit and the Japanese driver duly had to pit for a new nose. On rejoining, his Honda engine blew, but BAR still collected a podium result courtesy of Button. Barrichello, perhaps aggrieved to be so outclassed by his own team-mate yet again, was furious, calling Sato "amateur".

This time around the Renaults were outclassed and Jarno Trulli and Alonso had to make do with fourth and fifth, finishing half a minute down on Button and almost a full minute down on Michael Schumacher's winning Ferrari.

Perhaps one of the best drives in the race came from Giancarlo Fisichella, who managed to guide his Sauber around to sixth, not all that far behind the Renaults and just ahead of Mark Webber's Jaguar.

Michael Schumacher leads Takuma Sato and Jarno Trulli into the first corner where Sato and Trulli clashed, allowing Kimi Raikkonen through into second place

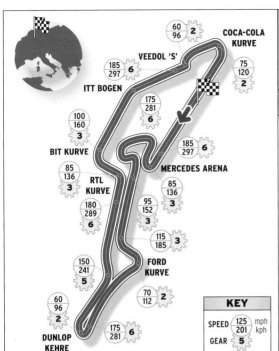

COCA-COLA KURVE 60/96 2

VEEDOL 'S' 185/297 6

ITT BOGEN

75/120 2

175/281 6

100/160 3

BIT KURVE 185/297 6

85/136 3 **RTL KURVE**

MERCEDES ARENA 85/136 3

180/289 6

95/152 3

115/185 3

FORD KURVE

150/241 5

70/112 2

60/96 2

175/281 6

DUNLOP KEHRE

KEY		
SPEED	125/201	mph/kph
GEAR	5	

POLE TIME
M Schumacher, 1m28.351s, 130.346mph/209.762kph

WINNER'S AVERAGE SPEED
124.379mph/200.159kph

FASTEST LAP
M Schumacher, 1m29.468s, 128.719mph/207.144kph

LAP LEADERS
M Schumacher, 1-8, 16-60; Alonso, 9; Sato, 10-11; Barrichello, 12-15

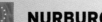

NURBURGRING ROUND 7

Date **30 May 2004** Laps **60** Distance **191.937 miles/308.879km**
Weather **Warm, dry and bright**

RACE RESULT

Position	Driver	Team	Result	Stops	Qualifying Time	Grid
1	Michael Schumacher	Ferrari	1h32m35.101s	3	1m28.351s	1
2	Rubens Barrichello	Ferrari	1h32m53.090s	2	1m29.353s	7
3	Jenson Button	BAR	1h32m57.634s	3	1m29.245s	5
4	Jarno Trulli	Renault	1h33m28.774s	3	1m29.135s	3
5	Fernando Alonso	Renault	1h33m36.088s	3	1m29.313s	6
6	Giancarlo Fisichella	Sauber	1h33m48.549s	2	no time	19
7	Mark Webber	Jaguar	1h33m51.307s	2	1m31.797s	14
8	Juan Pablo Montoya	Williams	59 laps	3	1m29.354s	8
9	Felipe Massa	Sauber	59 laps	2	1m31.982s	16
10	Nick Heidfeld	Jordan	59 laps	3	1m31.604s	13
11	Olivier Panis	Toyota	59 laps	3	1m29.697s	10
12	Christian Klien	Jaguar	59 laps	2	1m31.431s	12
13	Giorgio Pantano	Jordan	58 laps	4	1m31.979s	15
14	Gianmaria Bruni	Minardi	57 laps	3	1m34.022s	17
15	Zsolt Baumgartner	Minardi	57 laps	2	1m34.398s	18
R	Takuma Sato	BAR	47 laps/engine	4	1m28.986s	2
R	David Coulthard	McLaren	25 laps/engine	1	no time	20
R	Kimi Raikkonen	McLaren	9 laps/engine	1	1m29.137s	4
R	Ralf Schumacher	Williams	0 laps/accident	-	1m29.459s	9
R	Cristiano da Matta	Toyota	0 laps/accident	-	1m29.706s	11

TALKING POINT: RESHAPING QUALIFICATION

One of the recurring themes of last season was the constant quest for a qualifying format to replace the unpopular 45-minute sessions. An idea suggested by the teams was for a pair of 25-minute sessions in which drivers would be allowed to run with a low fuel load – and then be allowed to refuel for the race rather than having to start the race with the fuel that they had left over after qualifying. They also proposed that cars should all go out together rather than one after another, with each driver having a maximum of six laps in which to set his time.

A mechanic watches over Mark Webber's car in the pits

CANADIAN GP

Few drivers qualify sixth and come through to win. Yet this is exactly what Michael Schumacher did in Montreal, reaching the front without so much as passing a rival out on the circuit, and with brother Ralf as his shadow.

Michael Schumacher leads Juan Pablo Montoya early on, having passed the Colombian for fourth to work his way to the front and yet another victory

In a season that had produced six wins for Michael Schumacher from the first seven grands prix, it was widely hoped that some variety would be provided by another taking the chequered flag at the Circuit Gilles Villeneuve. When the six-time world champion qualified only sixth on the 20-car grid, there was hope that someone else would have a chance in the limelight. Yet, relentlessly, he forged his way to the front, the German taking his Ferrari to win number seven of the season, which was also his tally of wins in the Canadian Grand Prix.

Many were left wondering how this could have happened, how even the great Michael could have usurped the five drivers who had started ahead of him. Well, it went like this. Jarno Trulli was the first to lose out, the rear suspension on his Renault failing as he left the grid, apparently due to a driveshaft breaking. This elevated the Ferrari team leader by just one position, to fifth, as Ralf Schumacher led away

from pole position for Williams. Jenson Button held position for BAR in second, with Fernando Alonso powering ahead of Juan Pablo Montoya on the run to the first corner to occupy third.

With Button pitting as early as lap 12 – to reveal that he was on a three-stop strategy – and Ralf following him in a lap later, Alonso held the lead for a couple of laps in his Renault. However, Michael stayed out longest of all the leading quintet, stopping on lap 18, one later than team-mate Barrichello.

This late-stopping tactic clearly worked a treat, as not only did it elevate him to third place, but it also revealed that he was on a two-stop strategy. However, the pace of Barrichello in his wake, pressing hard to go by before those first pit stops, convinced Michael the Brazilian had made the better choice in opting for Bridgestone's softer tyre compound. As it was, Michael did what only Michael can and overcame this disadvantage through Montoya emerging

between the Ferrari duo after their first stops, delaying Barrichello sufficiently to let him ease clear. When all the other front-runners made their second of three pit stops, the Ferraris stayed out and ran one-two, with Barrichello really getting stuck into trying to pass Michael.

Had Barrichello not lost half a dozen seconds by skating wide after his second stop, he could easily have had a shot at winning. As it was, it let Michael escape and Ralf came through, too. Yet, Barrichello was to claim second place after all, as the Williams cars (and the Toyotas) were found to have illegal brake ducts and were thus disqualified.

Of the rest, Kimi Raikkonen's race was ruined when his McLaren ran over the white line exiting his first pit stop and collected a drive-through penalty. David Coulthard's race was blighted by being tipped into a spin by Jaguar's Christian Klien at the first corner, but the disqualifications at least raised him from ninth to sixth.

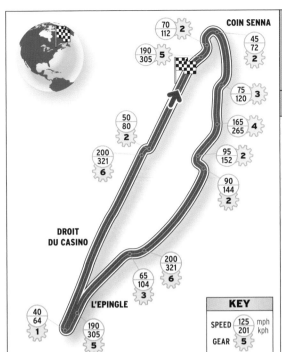

COIN SENNA

DROIT DU CASINO

L'EPINGLE

KEY		
SPEED	125 / 201	mph / kph
GEAR	5	

POLE TIME

R Schumacher, 1m12.175s, 135.168mph/217.521kph

WINNER'S AVERAGE SPEED

128.732mph/207.164kph

FASTEST LAP

Barrichello, 1m13.622s, 132.511mph/213.246kph

LAP LEADERS

R Schumacher, 1-14, 19-32, 47; Alonso, 15-16; M Schumacher, 17-18, 33-46, 48-70

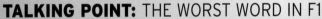

🇨🇦 MONTREAL ROUND 8

Date **13 June 2004** Laps **70** Distance **189.695 miles/305.270km**
Weather **Hot, dry and bright**

RACE RESULT

Position	Driver	Team	Result	Stops	Qualifying Time	Grid
1	Michael Schumacher	Ferrari	1h28m24.803s	2	1m13.355s	6
D	Ralf Schumacher	Williams	1h28m25.865s	3	1m12.175s	1
2	Rubens Barrichello	Ferrari	1h28m29.911s	2	1m13.562s	7
3	Jenson Button	BAR	1h28m45.212s	3	1m12.341s	2
D	Juan Pablo Montoya	Williams	1h28m46.003s	3	1m13.072s	4
4	Giancarlo Fisichella	Sauber	69 laps	2	1m14.674s	11
5	Kimi Raikkonen	McLaren	69 laps	5	1m13.595s	8
D	Cristiano da Matta	Toyota	69 laps	2	1m14.851s	12
6	David Coulthard	McLaren	69 laps	3	1m13.681s	9
D	Olivier Panis	Toyota	69 laps	2	1m14.891s	13
7	Timo Glock	Jordan	68 laps	2	1m16.323s	16
8	Nick Heidfeld	Jordan	68 laps	2	1m15.321s	15
9	Christian Klien	Jaguar	67 laps	4	1m14.532s	10
10	Zsolt Baumgartner	Minardi	66 laps	2	1m17.064s	18
R	Felipe Massa	Sauber	62 laps/suspension	3	no time	19
R	Takuma Sato	BAR	48 laps/engine	2	1m17.004s	17
R	Fernando Alonso	Renault	44 laps/driveshaft	1	1m13.308s	5
R	Gianmaria Bruni	Minardi	30 laps/gearbox	1	no time	20
R	Mark Webber	Jaguar	6 laps/ suspension	0	1m15.148s	14
R	Jarno Trulli	Renault	0 laps/suspension	0	1m13.023s	3

TALKING POINT: THE WORST WORD IN F1

Disqualification is a nasty word in any sport, but that is what both Williams and Toyota had to face up to in Montreal. Both teams were removed from the results for having brake ducts that exceeded the permitted width of 120mm inside the wheel, costing Ralf Schumacher second place and Juan Pablo Montoya fifth. For Toyota, Cristiano da Matta lost eighth place and Olivier Panis tenth. Sam Michael, in his first race as Williams' technical director, was deeply shocked. "It was unintentional, but there was no performance gain, as the inlet area wasn't any bigger."

Ralf Schumacher leads away, but it wasn't to be his day

UNITED STATES GP

Fans leaving the Indianapolis Motor Speedway after the race talked not of Michael Schumacher after yet another win, but of Ralf Schumacher's massive accident, of Rubens Barrichello for the relentless way in which he chased the world champion and, especially, of Takuma Sato for his effervescent attack.

Rubens Barrichello has spent years telling people that he is not the number two driver at Ferrari, but the equal number one. The trouble is Michael Schumacher has put him in the shade at almost every race since 2000.

At Indianapolis last year, though, the Brazilian raised his game and was the faster driver all weekend. However, there was just one moment when he was caught napping and that was all the time that Michael needed. This was when the safety car withdrew after the debris from a first-corner accident between Cristiano da Matta, Christian Klien, Giorgio Pantano, Felipe Massa and Gianmaria Bruni was cleared on lap six. It is thought that Michael was in front before they crossed the start line, the point at which the race was officially under way once more. However, having flashed onto the timing monitors that he had crossed the line first – and this would have meant a penalty – the positions were readjusted...

Michael's escape was helped by the second of two major accidents. The first befell Fernando Alonso, after his Renault suffered a blow-out going into Turn 1 – possibly as a result of debris. A lap later, it was Michael's brother Ralf who thumped the wall, doing so at the final corner as his Williams blew its left rear tyre. Michael pitted from the lead and was still ahead when he rejoined, but Barrichello lost ground and re-emerged sixth, behind Takuma Sato, Jenson Button, Mark Webber and Juan Pablo Montoya.

It took Barrichello until lap 35 to make it back to second, taking the lead seven laps later when Michael pitted. Rubens also had to pit again after some scorching laps.

It looked as though he had done enough to come out in front, but he failed by half a second and would have to content himself with attempting to pass Michael on that out lap. It didn't come off, though, and he had to settle

Michael Schumacher leads Rubens Barrichello as Ferrari controls the US GP. His brother wasn't so lucky

for yet another second place behind his overlord. Third place went to Sato. This was only the second-ever appearance of a Japanese driver on a Formula One podium – Aguri Suzuki had been there for Larrousse at Suzuka in 1990 – after a run full of brio as he fought and fought, overtaking Olivier Panis and Jarno Trulli as he advanced to that third position. Team-mate Button suffered his first retirement of the year and this left Trulli to finish fourth, just ahead of Panis, who was rewarded on his 150th Formula One outing with fifth place for Toyota, equalling his best performance for them.

McLaren showed an improvement in their last race before introducing the MP4-19B, with Kimi Raikkonen running third for a while before an extra pitstop, to have his hydraulics topped up, left him to finish sixth ahead of team-mate David Coulthard, both a lap down. Amazingly, there was only one other finisher, Zsolt Baumgartner. He may have been three laps adrift, but his perseverance gave Minardi a much-needed point after Giancarlo Fisichella's Sauber failed with seven laps to run.

The driver wearing the biggest scowl of all, though, was Montoya, who was black-flagged on lap 58 for an offence on the grid. Yes, he had raced for more than an hour before the officials saw fit to penalize him for not leaving the grid in the allotted time to change to his spare car.

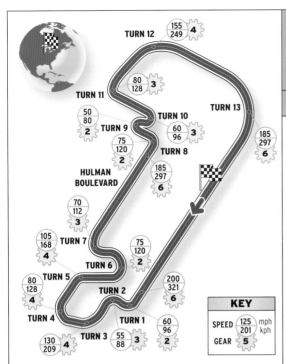

TURN 12 — 155/249 — 4
TURN 11 — 80/128 — 3
TURN 13 — 185/297 — 6
TURN 10 — 60/96 — 3
TURN 9 — 50/80 — 2
75/120 — 2
HULMAN BOULEVARD — 185/297 — 6
70/112 — 3
TURN 7 — 105/168 — 4
TURN 6 — 75/120 — 2
TURN 5 — 80/128 — 4
TURN 2 — 200/321 — 6
TURN 4 — TURN 1 — 60/96
TURN 3 — 55/88 — 2
130/209 — 4

KEY
SPEED — 125/201 — mph/kph
GEAR — 5

Date **20 June 2004** Laps **73** Distance **190.165 miles/306.027km**
Weather **Hot, dry and bright**

RACE RESULT

Position	Driver	Team	Result	Stops	Qualifying Time	Grid
1	Michael Schumacher	Ferrari	1h40m29.914s	2	1m10.400s	2
2	Rubens Barrichello	Ferrari	1h40m32.864s	2	1m10.223s	1
3	Takuma Sato	BAR	1h40m41.950s	2	1m10.601s	3
4	Jarno Trulli	Renault	1h41m04.458s	2	no time	20
5	Olivier Panis	Toyota	1h41m07.448s	2	1m11.167s	8
6	Kimi Raikkonen	McLaren	72 laps	3	1m11.137s	7
7	David Coulthard	McLaren	72 laps	3	1m12.026s	12
8	Zsolt Baumgartner	Minardi	70 laps	3	1m14.812s	19
9	Giancarlo Fisichella	Sauber	68 laps/hydraulics	2	1m12.470s	14
R	Mark Webber	Jaguar	72 laps/engine	2	1m11.286s	10
D	Juan Pablo Montoya	Williams	59 laps/infringement	2	1m11.062s	5
R	Nick Heidfeld	Jordan	43 laps/engine	2	1m13.147s	16
R	Jenson Button	BAR	26 laps/gearbox	1	1m10.820s	4
R	Cristiano da Matta	Toyota	17 laps/gearbox	2	1m11.691s	11
R	Ralf Schumacher	Williams	9 laps/accident	0	1m11.106s	6
R	Fernando Alonso	Renault	8 laps/accident	0	1m11.185s	9
R	Christian Klien	Jaguar	0 laps/accident	0	1m12.170s	13
R	Felipe Massa	Sauber	0 laps/accident	0	1m12.721s	15
R	Giorgio Pantano	Jordan	0 laps/accident	0	1m13.375s	17
R	Gianmaria Bruni	Minardi	0 laps/accident	0	1m14.010s	18

POLE TIME
Barrichello, 1m10.223s, 133.546mph/214.911kph

WINNER'S AVERAGE SPEED
113.529mph/182.699kph

FASTEST LAP
Barrichello, 1m10.399s, 133.207mph/214.366kph

LAP LEADERS
Barrichello, 1-5, 42-50; M Schumacher, 6-41, 51-73

TALKING POINT: CRACKS IN THE SYSTEM

Ralf Schumacher shocked onlookers with his massive accident into the concrete retaining wall at Turn 13. However, what shocked him even more than the fact that it took the medical crew three minutes to reach him (and that the field continued to stream through his debris for lap after lap behind the safety car) was that the medical specialists at the circuit failed to identify the fact he had sustained two cracked vertebrae in the massive impact. That he then flew home to Germany with these unstable wounds certainly didn't impress him and, ten days later, he talked of suing them.

Ralf Schumacher after his hard lesson in physics

FRENCH GP

When it comes to completely outwitting its rivals, Ferrari simply has no peer, as was proved by the four-stop strategy used by Michael Schumacher to notch up his ninth win of the season at Magny-Cours. A short pitlane, astute minds and the world champion's genius were simply too much for Fernando Alonso.

Fernando Alonso leads the field into the first corner ahead of Michael Schumacher, Trulli and Button

Speed is obvious, clever tactics less so, especially when everyone assumes that the drivers are all using either a three-stop or perhaps a two-stop strategy. So things looked set fair for Renault's Fernando Alonso to give the French manufacturer a victory on their home ground. But Ferrari put paid to that by playing a blinder and bringing Michael Schumacher in four times – something that has never intentionally been done before in dry conditions.

Alonso had excited the Renault hierarchy by qualifying on pole by almost a third of a second ahead of Michael's Ferrari, with McLaren's decision to enter its uprated car, the MP4-19B, for the first time being rewarded by David Coulthard lining up third, 0.016s behind Schumacher and 0.008s ahead of Jenson Button's BAR. Team-mate Kimi Raikkonen slipped up at the start of his qualifying lap and would start the race in ninth.

No car is quicker off the grid than a Renault, and so it proved again as Alonso shot off into the lead. Order was maintained behind them, except for Coulthard who fell back to fifth behind Jarno Trulli, up from fifth, and Button.

Alonso edged clear of Schumacher and was given a massive boost when the German made his first pit stop three laps earlier than he himself was planning to come in, meaning that his Renault had had the upper hand when running with more fuel on board. However, this optimism would have been based on the estimation that Michael was planning to stop three times, as he himself was, not four...

With Michael's second stop again three laps earlier than Alonso's, Renault still had no reason to believe anything other than that Michael was on a three-stopper. However, this put him into the lead for the first time. With Michael's third stop coming four laps earlier than Alonso's, there was still hope for the Spaniard, but Renault noted that the Ferrari hadn't taken on enough fuel for the rest of the race, meaning that although the German would have to make a fourth stop he would have two stints on a lighter fuel load than Alonso... It worked like a charm and, by flagfall, Michael was more than eight seconds ahead, having played a full role in tactician Luca Baldisserri's masterpiece.

On the final sector of the final lap, something extraordinary happened: Jarno Trulli appeared to fall asleep. Spotting this, Barrichello proved the ultimate opportunist to slip his Ferrari down the inside to snatch third place. He couldn't believe it and neither could Renault. The management were so furious at missing out on the chance of having both of its drivers on the podium at the team's home race that any talk of re-signing Trulli for 2005 was put on hold...

Button chased both across the line, with Coulthard and Raikkonen showing that McLaren had found reliability but not race speed as they finished sixth and seventh, with the final point going to Juan Pablo Montoya in a race that included a spin for the Colombian.

Marc Gene, standing in for the injured Ralf Schumacher at Williams, disappointed the team by finishing only tenth.

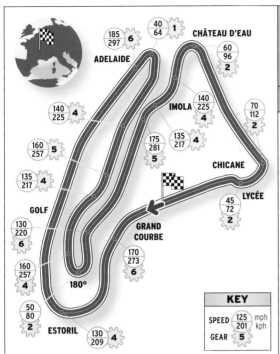

ADELAIDE
CHÂTEAU D'EAU
185/297 6
40/64 1
60/96 2
140/225 4
IMOLA
140/225 4
70/112 2
160/257 5
175/281 5
135/217 4
CHICANE
135/217 4
LYCÉE
45/72 2
GOLF
130/220 6
GRAND COURBE
170/273 6
160/257 4
180°
50/80 2
ESTORIL
130/209 4

KEY

SPEED	125 / 201	mph / kph
GEAR	5	

POLE TIME
Alonso, 1m13.698s, 133.892mph/215.469ph

WINNER'S AVERAGE SPEED
127.409mph/205.035kph

FASTEST LAP
M Schumacher, 1m15.377s, 130.910mph/210.669kph

LAP LEADERS
Alonso, 1–32, 43–46; M Schumacher, 33–42, 47–70

MAGNY-COURS ROUND 10

Date **4 July 2004** Laps **70** Distance **191.870 miles/308.771km**
Weather **Very hot, dry and bright**

RACE RESULT

Position	Driver	Team	Result	Stops	Qualifying Time	Grid
1	Michael Schumacher	Ferrari	1h30m18.133s	4	1m13.971s	2
2	Fernando Alonso	Renault	1h30m26.462s	3	1m13.698s	1
3	Rubens Barrichello	Ferrari	1h30m49.755s	3	1m14.478s	10
4	Jarno Trulli	Renault	1h30m50.215s	3	1m14.070s	5
5	Jenson Button	BAR	1h30m50.617s	3	1m13.995s	4
6	David Coulthard	McLaren	1h30m53.653s	3	1m13.987s	3
7	Kimi Raikkonen	McLaren	1h30m54.363s	3	1m14.346s	9
8	Juan Pablo Montoya	Williams	1h31m01.552s	3	1m14.172s	6
9	Mark Webber	Jaguar	1h31m10.527s	3	1m14.798s	12
10	Marc Gene	Williams	1h31m16.299s	3	1m14.275s	8
11	Christian Klien	Jaguar	69 laps	3	1m15.065s	13
12	Giancarlo Fisichella	Sauber	69 laps	3	1m16.177s	15
13	Felipe Massa	Sauber	69 laps	2	1m16.200s	16
14	Cristiano da Matta	Toyota	69 laps	3	1m14.553s	11
15	Olivier Panis	Toyota	68 laps	3	1m15.130s	14
16	Nick Heidfeld	Jordan	68 laps	4	1m16.807s	17
17	Giorgio Pantano	Jordan	67 laps	4	1m17.462s	18
18	Gianmaria Bruni	Minardi	65 laps/oil leak	3	1m17.913s	19
R	Zsolt Baumgartner	Minardi	31 laps/accident	2	1m18.247s	20
R	Takuma Sato	BAR	15 laps/engine	1	1m14.240s	7

TALKING POINT: ENOUGH IS ENOUGH

In the run-up to the French GP, FIA president Max Mosley shocked everyone by announcing that he was standing down from his role not at the end of 2005 as planned but a year early, having "had enough of sitting in long meetings, particularly with the Formula One and World Rally Championship teams, where people agree things and then go away and change their minds". Minardi supremo Paul Stoddart considered it a body blow to the sport, but McLaren boss Ron Dennis said that he reckoned Mosley quit because he feared losing the next FIA presidential elections.

FIA President Max Mosley in the full glare of publicity

BRITISH GP

No one was too surprised when Michael Schumacher made it ten wins from 11 starts, but there was just as much talk immediately after the race about McLaren's refound form that helped Kimi Raikkonen split the Ferraris, and Jarno Trulli's massive accident at Priory, from which he walked away unharmed.

Anyone who watched Kimi Raikkonen's opening lap might have thought that they needed their eyes checked, for not only was a McLaren leading a grand prix, but it was also almost 3.5s clear of Rubens Barrichello's Ferrari after the first lap. He extended that gap on the second, but then it started to diminish. In a matter of minutes, though, Raikkonen had proved that the MP4-19B was a comprehensive step forward from the ill-fated MP4-19 and that Michelins were the tyres to have for the first few laps. It also proved that the Bridgestone tyres used by Ferrari were the better ones thereafter in the unseasonably cool weather.

Michael Schumacher had started fourth and was stuck there, behind Jenson Button's BAR, but not threatening it. The reason why became clear after 13 laps when all the frontrunners bar Michael made the first of their stops and he stayed out, making the most of the clear track ahead of him. Ferrari's two-stop strategy for Michael paid dividends as Raikkonen found himself stuck in traffic. Precious time was lost and so Michael was able to pit and vault from fourth to first without even having to overtake another car.

He then led with ease, but a violent incident hauled him back into the battle. Jarno Trulli had slammed backwards into the tyrewall approaching Priory at 170mph then rotated a few times before rolling to a halt in the gravel trap. He stepped out unharmed, reckoning that his left rear suspension had collapsed. This brought out the safety car which triggered a mass rush to the pits for what was, effectively, a free pit stop. Already fuelled to the finish, Michael must have been fuming as his advantage was wiped out. He feared that Raikkonen might be able to outrun him on his new rubber, especially over the first lap after the safety car was called back in. However, there were two cars between the world

champion and the Finn – Cristiano da Matta's Toyota and Christian Klien's Jaguar – and they were just enough to delay Raikkonen catching Michael until his tyres were no longer superior. Thus Kimi's best shot was thwarted. Last year he would have been petulant at finishing second, but the taciturn Finn even came close to smiling, so marked had McLaren's progress been. Certainly, Michael had won with ease, the two-stop strategy he was asked to run a masterpiece, but Raikkonen's first podium of the year was no fluke and team boss Ron Dennis had high hopes that Hockenheim would yield even greater results.

The home crowd's hopes of a British driver on the podium came to nought as Barrichello ended up third, having got past Jenson Button after the second round of pitstops.

Juan Pablo Montoya wrestled his Williams around to fifth place, but it was the driver in sixth, namely Giancarlo Fisichella, who took the plaudits.

He had started 20th after failing to set a time in qualifying. Then, by running a two-stop strategy with a very long first stint, found himself sixth and stayed there to finish ahead of David Coulthard and Mark Webber.

Kimi Raikkonen hit the front at Silverstone in the updated McLaren, but he had to cede to Schumacher

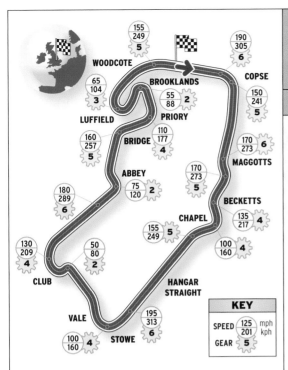

WOODCOTE
155 / 249 / 5
65 / 104 / 3
BROOKLANDS
55 / 88 / 2
PRIORY
LUFFIELD
110 / 177 / 4
BRIDGE
160 / 257 / 5
ABBEY
75 / 120 / 2
180 / 289 / 6
170 / 273 / 5
50 / 80 / 2
130 / 209 / 4
155 / 249 / 5
CHAPEL
CLUB
HANGAR STRAIGHT
195 / 313 / 6
VALE
100 / 160 / 4
STOWE
190 / 305 / 6
COPSE
150 / 241 / 5
170 / 273 / 6
MAGGOTTS
170 / 273 / 5
BECKETTS
135 / 217 / 4
100 / 160 / 4

KEY

SPEED	125 / 201	mph kph
GEAR	5	

POLE TIME
Raikkonen, 1m18.233s, 147.004mph/236.569kph

WINNER'S AVERAGE SPEED
135.716mph/218.404kph

FASTEST LAP
M Schumacher, 1m18.739s, 146.059mph/235.049kph

LAP LEADERS
Raikkonen, 1-11; M Schumacher, 12-60

RACE RESULT

Position	Driver	Team	Result	Stops	Qualifying Time	Grid
1	Michael Schumacher	Ferrari	1h24m42.700s	2	1m18.710s	4
2	Kimi Raikkonen	McLaren	1h24m44.830s	3	1m18.233s	1
3	Rubens Barrichello	Ferrari	1h24m45.814s	3	1m18.305s	2
4	Jenson Button	BAR	1h24m53.383s	3	1m18.580s	3
5	Juan Pablo Montoya	Williams	1h24m54.873s	3	1m19.378s	8
6	Giancarlo Fisichella	Sauber	1h24m55.588s	2	No time	20
7	David Coulthard	McLaren	1h25m02.368s	3	1m19.148s	7
8	Mark Webber	Jaguar	1h25m06.401s	2	1m20.004s	10
9	Felipe Massa	Sauber	1h25m06.723s	2	1m20.202s	11
10	Fernando Alonso	Renault	1h25m07.535s	3	1m18.811s	6
11	Takuma Sato	BAR	1h25m16.436s	2	1m19.688s	9
12	Marc Gene	Williams	1h25m17.003s	3	1m20.335s	13
13	Cristiano da Matta	Toyota	59 laps	2	1m20.545s	14
14	Christian Klien	Jaguar	59 laps	2	1m21.559s	15
15	Nick Heidfeld	Jordan	59 laps	2	1m22.677s	17
16	Gianmaria Bruni	Minardi	56 laps	4	1m23.437s	18
R	Giorgio Pantano	Jordan	47 laps/accident	2	1m22.458s	16
R	Jarno Trulli	Renault	39 laps/accident	2	1m18.715s	5
R	Zsolt Baumgartner	Minardi	29 laps/engine	2	1m24.117s	19
R	Olivier Panis	Toyota	16 laps/extinguisher	1	1m20.335s	12

TALKING POINT: THE BATTLE OF BRITAIN

A pre-race publicity stunt to help promote the British GP by running F1 cars on the streets of London was turned against Silverstone. The Mayor of London, Ken Livingstone, manipulated the event so it became a pitch for a grand prix in London, perhaps as early as 2006, perhaps in addition to the race at Silverstone, but perhaps in place of it. But Bernie Ecclestone said he would be happy to keep the race at Silverstone if they found a promoter and signed a new contract, although the two parties appeared some way apart in their financial discussions.

Nigel Mansell beats the traffic jams in Regent St, London

GERMAN GP

Michael Schumacher raced to victory in his home grand prix, but the real winner was Jenson Button, who battled his way from 13th on the grid to finish second, entertaining the huge crowd every metre of the way.

Fernando Alonso holds off Jenson Button as the BAR driver presses him for second place in his pursuit of Michael Schumacher. It was his best drive of the year

If you look at the record books you will see that this was Michael Schumacher's 81st win. It was a result that sent his fans home happy, but it wasn't a win that will stand out in years to come, simply because he has had so many that it is increasingly hard to recall one from another. Had the driver in second, Jenson Button, come away with the victor's laurels it would be easy to remember a few years from now as not only would it have been the Englishman's first win on the sport's biggest stage, but it would have been one of the most remarkable drives of the modern era.

Drivers don't win from way back down the grid, you see. Sure, John Watson managed the unimaginable when he started 22nd at the US West Grand Prix at Long Beach in 1983 and managed to pass car after car to win, but this was the best reversal of qualifying positions since Schumacher climbed from 16th to win the 1995 Belgian Grand Prix. Button had not been slow in qualifying. Indeed, he had only been slower than Schumacher and Juan Pablo

Montoya's Williams, but his Honda engine had blown in Friday practice and thus he'd fallen foul of the rule that states that any driver whose car requires an engine change will be demoted ten places down the grid.

Ferrari fans revelled in Schumacher's progress in the race, especially as Montoya was removed from the equation before the first corner after a slow start, dropping to seventh behind Fernando Alonso, who powered his Renault past the all-McLaren second row, with Jarno Trulli and Mark Webber also making up ground. Their delight was tempered by Rubens Barrichello having to pit at the end of the opening lap after knocking his nose off following a clash with David Coulthard's McLaren. The Scot was to suffer further when he damaged his car's nose by running over debris on the track. It was even worse for his team-mate Kimi Raikkonen, though, as the debris that affected Coulthard's car came from the McLaren of the Finn who endured a huge crash after his rear wing failed...

This all helped Button, but he wasn't willing to wait for charity, overtaking Cristiano da Matta and Christian Klien before the first round of pit-stops and even leading briefly as he stayed out longest of all on his first set of tyres. The Englishman's pace meant that he was fifth when the order settled down again and he then set about passing Montoya. A long second stint saw him lead again, but, when the dust settled, his flying pace left him only third behind Schumacher and Alonso. With Alonso struggling from a handling imbalance as a result of hitting Raikkonen's debris, Button was able to pass him after the final round of pit stops. That left just Schumacher ahead of him. And the gap was down to 8.5s by flagfall. No wonder he later described his drive as "by far the best of my Formula One career".

Williams used a second replacement for the injured Ralf Schumacher, with Antonio Pizzonia having a steady run to seventh place, two places and 19 seconds behind Montoya.

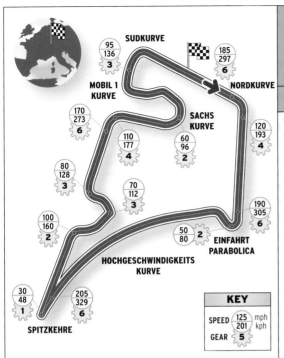

HOCKENHEIM ROUND 12

Date **25 July 2004** Laps **66** Distance **187.590 miles/301.883km**
Weather **Hot, dry and bright**

RACE RESULT

Position	Driver	Team	Result	Stops	Qualifying Time	Grid
1	Michael Schumacher	Ferrari	1h23m54.848s	3	1m13.306s	1
2	Jenson Button	BAR	1h24m03.236s	3	1m13.674s	13*
3	Fernando Alonso	Renault	1h24m11.199s	3	1m13.874s	5
4	David Coulthard	McLaren	1h24m14.079s	3	1m13.821s	4
5	Juan Pablo Montoya	Williams	1h24m17.903s	3	1m13.668s	2
6	Mark Webber	Jaguar	1h24m35.956s	3	1m14.802s	11
7	Antonio Pizzonia	Williams	1h24m36.804s	3	1m14.556s	10
8	Takuma Sato	BAR	1h24m41.690s	3	1m14.287s	8
9	Giancarlo Fisichella	Sauber	1h25m01.950s	2	1m15.395s	14
10	Christian Klien	Jaguar	1h25m03.426s	3	1m15.011s	12
11	Jarno Trulli	Renault	1h25m05.106s	3	1m114.134s	6
12	Rubens Barrichello	Ferrari	1h25m08.100s	3	1m14.278s	7
13	Felipe Massa	Sauber	65 laps	2	1m15.616s	16
14	Olivier Panis	Toyota	65 laps	4	1m14.368s	9**
15	Giorgio Pantano	Jordan	63 laps	4	1m16.192s	17
16	Zsolt Baumgartner	Minardi	62 laps	3	1m18.400s	20
17	Gianmaria Bruni	Minardi	62 laps	3	1m18.055s	19
R	Nick Heidfeld	Jordan	42 laps/handling	3	1m16.310s	18
R	Cristiano da Matta	Toyota	38 laps/puncture	2	1m15.454s	15
R	Kimi Raikkonen	McLaren	13 laps/accident	1	1m13.690s	3

* Moved 10 places back down the grid as his car had an engine change earlier in the meeting.

** Started from the pitline.

POLE TIME

M Schumacher, 1m13.306s, 139.582mph/224.625kph

WINNER'S AVERAGE SPEED

134.130mph/215.851kph

FASTEST LAP

Raikkonen, 1m13.780s, 138.685mph/223.182kph

LAP LEADERS

M Schumacher, 1-10, 15-28, 35-47, 51-66; Raikkonen, 11; Button, 12-14, 30-34, 48-50; Alonso, 29

TALKING POINT: ALL HOLDS BAR-RED

"No FT, no comment" is a catchphrase used to good effect by the *Financial Times*. For BAR in the summer of 2004, it was a case of "FTT, plenty of comment" as they met stiff resistance to their Front Torque Transfer braking system. Its aim was to eliminate locking up during braking by transferring torque loads between the wheels. When the cars went out with it in Friday's free practice, rival teams complained and FIA technical delegate Charlie Whiting declared it illegal. BAR sought clarification, but the system was subsequently rejected by the International Court of Appeal.

Anthony Davidson was one to use FTT in Germany

HUNGARIAN GP

Ferrari's domination of the World Championship was near complete, but their victory in Hungary left their rivals reeling and wishing they had tyres that suited them as well as the Bridgestones seemed to suit Ferraris.

What a difference a year makes. Not to the triumphal passage of Michael Schumacher towards another title, but to the outcome of this race. On a circuit that offers little option for race tactics because it is so hard for drivers to overtake even the slowest of backmarkers around its twists and turns – everyone opts for a three-stop strategy – a good grid position is essential and, to achieve that, a competitive set of tyres is a must. In 2003, Ferrari's prancing horse had slowed to a walk, with Michael Schumacher having finished the race a lapped eighth. A lack of competitive rubber was the problem, as on that occasion Michelin got it just right and Fernando Alonso drove a blinding race in his Renault to secure his first grand prix win. Twelve months on, and the tables had been turned.

Bridgestone had worked flat out over the close season – using the debacle of the 2003 race as an incentive – and nowhere was their input rewarded as much as in the heat and dust of the Hungaroring. Schumacher got the most out of their new rear tyre to qualify fastest, with Rubens Barrichello next up. Then came BAR, with Takuma Sato this time ahead of Button, albeit half a second down on pole. Alonso was 0.85 seconds adrift in fifth. Less than happy, at least he had cause to think that he might reach the podium, which is more than could be said of the McLaren duo, with Kimi Raikkonen tenth and David Coulthard languishing in 12th after the team opted for the harder Michelin tyre for both qualifying and the race.

A drop in temperature for qualifying may have assisted Ferrari, but they needed no help in the race as they never ran lower than first and second, with Schumacher winning by 4.7 seconds. This showed that he didn't have matters all his own way, but the fact that the best of the rest – Alonso's fast-starting Renault – was 40 seconds adrift shows how complete the Italian team's domination was. In truth, Ferrari's drivers did not even look as though they had been trying that hard. Schumacher claimed another record: it was his 12th win of the season, one more than he had managed in 2002, with five races remaining. Ferrari put its name down for another record, too, claiming its sixth consecutive constructors' championship crown.

Alonso was left to appreciate what the Ferrari drivers must have felt in 2003 when he waltzed clear, and he was almost beside himself with fury at Michelin for not matching Bridgestone. The French tyre manufacturer's Pierre Dupasquier was less than impressed with this outburst and suggested that perhaps Renault might want to produce a more competitive car...

Juan Pablo Montoya attempted to keep Alonso in check, this time running with a regular nose on his Williams in place of the twin-finned "walrus" nose, but he simply did not have the speed and had to settle for fourth ahead of a slow-starting Button. Dropped by Toyota for a supposed lack of form, Cristiano da Matta was at home in Curitiba, his seat at Toyota filled by fellow Brazilian Ricardo Zonta who had been promoted from the team's third-driver role. In turn, Zonta's seat was handed on to Toyota protege Ryan Briscoe.

Michael Schumacher takes the chequered flag to all but wrap up the 2004 Formula One title, his seventh

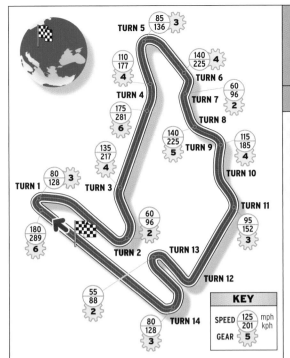

TURN 5 85/136 • 3
110/177 • 4
140/225 • 4
TURN 6
TURN 4
60/96 • 2
TURN 7
175/281 • 6
TURN 8
140/225 • 5
TURN 9
115/185 • 4
135/217 • 4
TURN 10
80/128 • 3
TURN 1
TURN 3
TURN 11
60/96 • 2
95/152 • 3
180/289 • 6
TURN 2
TURN 13
TURN 12
55/88 • 2
80/128 • 3
TURN 14

KEY
| SPEED | 125 / 201 | mph / kph |
| GEAR | 5 | |

POLE TIME
M Schumacher, 1m19.146s, 123.828mph/199.272kph

WINNER'S AVERAGE SPEED
119.805mph/192.799kph

FASTEST LAP
M Schumacher, 1m19.071s, 123.945mph/199.461kph

LAP LEADERS
M Schumacher, 1-70

HUNGARORING ROUND 13
Date **15 August 2004** Laps **70** Distance **190.564 miles/306.669km**
Weather **Hot, dry and bright**

RACE RESULT

Position	Driver	Team	Result	Stops	Qualifying Time	Grid
1	Michael Schumacher	Ferrari	1h35m26.131s	3	1m19.146s	1
2	Rubens Barrichello	Ferrari	1h35m30.827s	3	1m19.323s	2
3	Fernando Alonso	Renault	1h36m10.730s	3	1m19.996s	5
4	Juan Pablo Montoya	Williams	1h36m28.744s	3	1m20.199s	7
5	Jenson Button	BAR	1h36m33.570s	3	1m19.700s	4
6	Takuma Sato	BAR	69 laps	3	1m19.693s	3
7	Antonio Pizzonia	Williams	69 laps	3	1m20.170s	6
8	Giancarlo Fisichella	Sauber	69 laps	3	1m20.324s	8
9	David Coulthard	McLaren	69 laps	3	1m20.897s	12
10	Mark Webber	Jaguar	69 laps	3	1m20.730s	11
11	Olivier Panis	Toyota	69 laps	3	1m21.068s	13
12	Nick Heidfeld	Jordan	68 laps	3	1m22.180s	16
13	Christian Klien	Jaguar	68 laps	3	1m21.118s	14
14	Gianmaria Bruni	Minardi	66 laps	3	1m24.679s	19
15	Zsolt Baumgartner	Minardi	65 laps	3	1m24.329s	18
R	Giorgio Pantano	Jordan	48 laps/gearbox	3	1m22.356s	17
R	Jarno Trulli	Renault	41 laps/engine	3	1m20.411s	9
R	Ricardo Zonta	Toyota	31 laps/electronics	2	1m21.135s	15
R	Felipe Massa	Sauber	21 laps/brakes	2	no time	20
R	Kimi Raikkonen	McLaren	13 laps/electronics	1	1m20.570s	10

TALKING POINT: BUTTONED-UP

Jenson Button was tight-lipped in Hungary. After his stunning drive at Hockenheim, he was always going to be in demand, but the reason the media was hounding him was that he was in the middle of a tug-of-war between BAR and Williams for his services in 2005, with BAR believing that it had taken up its option with him in July and Button's management saying that BAR's option was no longer valid. It was thus in the hands of the lawyers and heading for the Contracts Recognition Board, and so beyond the understanding of the fans who thought that he had agreed to race on with BAR.

Button offers a rare smile during a troubled weekend

BELGIAN GP

This race had more twists than any other grand prix that was run in 2004. At the end of it all, Kimi Raikkonen had become only the second driver to beat Michael Schumacher all year; Schuey himself was crowned champion yet again and the driver of the safety car notched up more laps than many of the drivers...

Huge efforts have been made to make qualifying more of a lottery. For all this, the weather did it for them. The amount of rain kept changing, but Jarno Trulli hit the sweet spot and claimed pole for Renault and Michelin ahead of Michael Schumacher, Ferrari and Bridgestone. Other notable infiltrators were David Coulthard – with the fourth-fastest time behind Fernando Alonso – and Giancarlo Fisichella, who was fifth.

With the title all but his, Michael Schumacher did not really need to take any risks, but he would have wanted a better start as he lost out to Alonso before La Source. Then Coulthard dived up his inside to claim third, but

everything exploded behind them as the pack was bunched by Fisichella's slow getaway. Mark Webber hit Rubens Barrichello and damaged the Ferrari's rear wing. Then Fisichella was hit by Olivier Panis and Felipe Massa tapped Kimi Raikkonen. The Finn was propelled out of the melee and leapt from tenth to fifth as Jenson Button was hit by Antonio Pizzonia and clipped Massa, with Nick Heidfeld clouting Pizzonia. Then, as Takuma Sato powered through Eau Rouge, Webber, minus his front wing, clattered into the rear of the BAR, spinning it and taking out Gianmaria Bruni and Giorgio Pantano. It came as no surprise that the safety car was deployed...

When it withdrew, Raikkonen made the most of the Michelins' ability to come up to temperature and passed Schumacher into Eau Rouge. Juan Pablo Montoya also demoted the German, around the outside of the reprofiled Bus Stop.

Then Raikkonen passed Coulthard for third. Within a handful of laps, Raikkonen was in front after Trulli pitted from the lead and Alonso spun on his own oil. Then Coulthard's run in second was thwarted when he suffered one of many Michelin blow-outs.

Schumacher got ahead of Montoya in the first round of pitstops, so the Colombian was in attack mode when he rejoined and soon tipped Trulli into a spin at the Bus Stop; this hobbled the Italian's car and allowed team-mate Pizzonia to move into third as he regathered his own momentum.

Button had climbed to fifth after being forced to pit for a new nose, but he had a 200mph blow-out into Les Combes and took out Zsolt Baumgartner's Minardi as he spun. With debris everywhere, the safety car came out again, offering Schumacher and Montoya "free" pit stops – as Raikkonen had pitted a lap earlier – and the chance to wipe out the Finn's 12s lead.

Pizzonia lost third place when his gearbox failed and Williams' day of promise ended when Montoya had a blow-out with seven laps to go. This helped to promote Barrichello from almost a lap down to third place...

Soon afterwards, Coulthard ran along the barriers at 180mph after a failed move on Christian Klien. This brought out the safety car for the third time and the race's final incident came when Ricardo Zonta, who had climbed from 20th to fourth, suffered an engine failure with three laps to go. As a result, Massa claimed his best result, fourth, not bad since he, like Barrichello, had had to pit for a new rear wing.

Kimi Raikkonen keeps ahead of Michael Schumacher to take resurgent McLaren to its only win of 2004

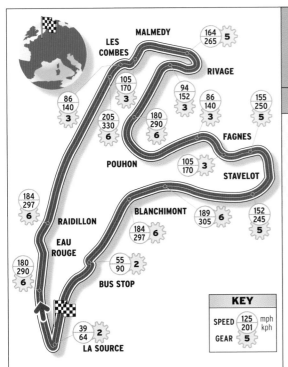

POLE TIME
Trulli, 1m56.232s, 134.204mph/215.970kph

WINNER'S AVERAGE SPEED
123.549mph/198.823kph

FASTEST LAP
Raikkonen, 1m45.108s, 148.407mph/238.827kph

LAP LEADERS
Trulli, 1-9; Alonso, 10-11; Raikkonen, 12-13, 17-29, 31-44; Montoya, 14; M Schumacher, 15, 30; Pizzonia, 16

SPA-FRANCORCHAMPS ROUND 14

Date **29 August 2004** Laps **44** Distance **190.652 miles/306.810km**
Weather **Warm, dry and bright**

RACE RESULT

Position	Driver	Team	Result	Stops	Qualifying Time	Grid
1	**Kimi Raikkonen**	McLaren	1h32m35.274s	2	1m59.635s	10
2	**Michael Schumacher**	Ferrari	1h32m38.406s	2	1m56.304s	2
3	**Rubens Barrichello**	Ferrari	1h32m39.645s	3	1m58.175s	6
4	**Felipe Massa**	Sauber	1h32m47.778s	4	1m59.008s	8
5	**Giancarlo Fisichella**	Sauber	1h32m49.378s	2	1m58.040s	5
6	**Christian Klien**	Jaguar	1h32m49.888s	3	2m01.246s	13
7	**David Coulthard**	McLaren	1h32m53.244s	3	1m57.990s	4
8	**Olivier Panis**	Toyota	1h32m53.967s	3	1m59.552s	9
9	**Jarno Trulli**	Renault	1h32m55.389s	2	1m56.232s	1
10	**Ricardo Zonta**	Toyota	41 laps/engine	2	2m03.895s	20
11	**Nick Heidfeld**	Jordan	40 laps	5	2m02.645s	16
R	**Juan Pablo Montoya**	Williams	37 laps/suspension	2	1m59.681s	11
R	**Antonio Pizzonia**	Williams	31 laps/gearbox	2	2m.01.447s	14
R	**Jenson Button**	BAR	29 laps/accident	2	2m00.237s	12
R	**Zsolt Baumgartner**	Minardi	28 laps/accident	2	2m03.303s	18
R	**Fernando Alonso**	Renault	11 laps/accident	0	1m56.686s	3
R	**Mark Webber**	Jaguar	0 laps/accident	0	1m58.729s	7
R	**Takuma Sato**	BAR	0 laps/accident	0	2m01.813s	15
R	**Gianmaria Bruni**	Minardi	0 laps/accident	0	2m02.651s	17
R	**Giorgio Pantano**	Jordan	0 laps/accident	0	2m03.833s	19

TALKING POINT: LUCKY SEVEN

Seven is many people's lucky number. Well, it might be Michael Schumacher's too, not that he's the sort of person who needs one, for his second place in the Belgian GP brought him his seventh world title after the most unlikely of races. The fact that he landed the title at Spa-Francorchamps is fitting, too, as it was here, of course, that he made his F1 debut in 1991, standing in at Jordan for the jailed Bertrand Gachot. Emphasizing the factor of seven, the race was also Ferrari's 700th World Championship start, giving the outcome added significance.

Schumacher celebrates his seventh title among friends

ITALIAN GP

This was a topsy-turvy race with a fast-drying track confusing the drivers at the start and then Jenson Button leading for most of the race before Ferrari found another gear and Rubens Barrichello claimed a rare victory.

Jenson Button led for much of the race before the Ferrari duo swept by late on after the circuit dried

A Ferrari one-two finish at Monza in a season of Ferrari domination won't have come as much of a surprise, but the way in which it was achieved did. After all, pole-sitter Rubens Barrichello looked to have messed up by opting for intermediate tyres as the track dried in the countdown to the race. Meanwhile, Michael Schumacher spun to the tail of the field on lap one. With BAR and Renault seemingly in control, it looked as though the *tifosi*'s day was going to be spoiled, but then through came the red cavalry.

Barrichello was helped clear by a first chicane sort-out that had his more illustrious team-mate running across the kerbs and having to wait for Juan Pablo Montoya to get the power down before rejoining the race or running the risk of a penalty for trying to find an advantage. Then Michael couldn't find any grip on his dry-weather tyres – he had watched what Barrichello fitted on the grid and then opted for the opposite – and slid wide into Jenson Button's BAR. By the time he'd gathered his Ferrari together, he was down in 15th place. He was more fortunate than Olivier Panis, though, who was caught out in the chain reaction behind him and put himself out of the race by

hitting Antonio Pizzonia's Williams. Barrichello was 6.9s clear at the end of the opening lap, one of the biggest first-lap advantages ever, but he wasn't to be in front for long as the track was soon all but dry and so he pitted for dry tyres after just five laps. Now Fernando Alonso was in front for Renault, with Barrichello out of pit sequence and down in ninth, two places ahead of Michael. The *tifosi* were despondent, but they needn't have been.

Alonso came in for his first scheduled stop on lap ten, with Button taking over at the front after working his way forward from sixth and staying out for a further four laps, one more than Montoya and team-mate Takuma Sato. Kimi Raikkonen had been fourth, but he parked his McLaren with yet another engine failure. At this point, Michael was 30s behind the race leader, Button, but was flying, making it up to fourth. He fell back to tenth after his pit stop, but it was now clear that the Michelin-shod teams were struggling for grip. And so the Ferraris came back into the equation.

Button stayed in front until his final stop on lap 34, ceding the lead to Michael, who then fell to fourth when he pitted. With his second stop long behind him, Barrichello thus took the lead, but he needed one more stop.

Such was the pace of the Ferraris that he was still in the lead when he re-emerged, by a fraction from Michael, who had passed Button for second on that same lap. With the title already in Michael's hands, there would be no orders for Barrichello to let him through and so the Brazilian claimed his first win of the year. Button was left third, with Alonso spinning away what would have been fourth just as Michael caught him, a place that was taken by Sato to help BAR vault past Renault into second place in the constructors' rankings.

The most dramatic moment was Minardi's, though, as Gianmaria Bruni's car was engulfed in flames as a result of a pit fire.

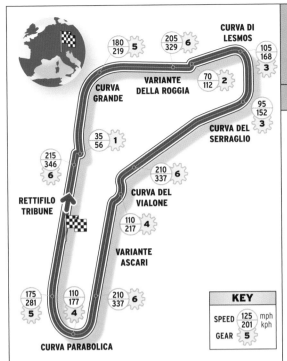

MONZA ROUND 14

Date **12 September 2004** Laps **53** Distance **190.800 miles/307.049km**
Weather **Warm but overcast following rain**

RACE RESULT

Position	Driver	Team	Result	Stops	Qualifying Time	Grid
1	Rubens Barrichello	Ferrari	1h15m18.448s	3	1m20.089s	1
2	Michael Schumacher	Ferrari	1h15m19.795s	2	1m20.637s	3
3	Jenson Button	BAR	1h15m28.645s	2	1m20.786s	6
4	Takuma Sato	BAR	1h15m33.818s	2	1m20.715s	5
5	Juan Pablo Montoya	Williams	1h15m50.800s	2	1m20.620s	2
6	David Coulthard	McLaren	1h15m51.887s	1	1m21.049s	10*
7	Antonio Pizzonia	Williams	1h15m52.200s	2	1m20.888s	8
8	Giancarlo Fisichella	Sauber	1h15m53.879s	2	1m22.239s	15
9	Mark Webber	Jaguar	1h16m15.209s	2	1m21.602s	12
10	Jarno Trulli	Renault	1h16m24.674s	2	1m21.027s	9
11	Ricardo Zonta	Toyota	1h16m40.979s	2	1m21.520s	11
12	Felipe Massa	Sauber	52 laps	2	1m22.287s	16
13	Christian Klien	Jaguar	52 laps	3	1m21.989s	14
14	Nick Heidfeld	Jordan	52 laps	2	1m22.301s	17
15	Zsolt Baumgartner	Minardi	50 laps	2	1m24.808s	19
R	Fernando Alonso	Renault	40 laps/accident	2	1m20.645s	4
R	Giorgio Pantano	Jordan	33 laps/accident	2	1m23.239s	18
R	Gianmaria Bruni	Minardi	29 laps/pit fire	2	1m24.940s	20
R	Kimi Raikkonen	McLaren	13 laps/engine	0	1m20.877s	7
R	Olivier Panis	Toyota	0 laps/accident	0	1m21.841s	13

* Denotes started from the pitline.

Circuit labels

CURVA DI LESMOS
180 / 219 — 5
205 / 329 — 6
105 / 168 — 3
VARIANTE DELLA ROGGIA
70 / 112 — 2
CURVA GRANDE
95 / 152 — 3
CURVA DEL SERRAGLIO
35 / 56 — 1
215 / 346 — 6
210 / 337 — 6
CURVA DEL VIALONE
RETTIFILO TRIBUNE
110 / 217 — 4
VARIANTE ASCARI
175 / 281 — 5
110 / 177 — 4
210 / 337 — 6
CURVA PARABOLICA

KEY
SPEED 125 mph / 201 kph
GEAR 5

POLE TIME
Barrichello, 1m20.089s, 161.820mph/260.412kph

WINNER'S AVERAGE SPEED
151.854mph/244.374kph

FASTEST LAP
Barrichello, 1m21.046s, 159.899mph/257.321kph

LAP LEADERS
Barrichello, 1-4, 37-53; Alonso, 5-10; Button, 11-34; M Schumacher, 35-36

TALKING POINT: TRULLI MADLY DEEPLY

Jarno Trulli already knew he would not be racing for Renault in 2005, with a deal due to be announced with Toyota. However, it came as a shock when the team decided to drop him for the final three races of the season. Certainly, his results since winning at Monaco had dropped away and he was convinced something was wrong with his chassis, but he was ranked fourth in the championship, one point ahead of team-mate Fernando Alonso. However, he was out after Monza, with 1997 world champion Jacques Villeneuve due to step out of retirement to replace him.

Jarno Trulli went mysteriously off the boil at Monza

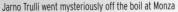

CHINESE GP

Rubens Barrichello had never scored back-to-back wins before, so he was delighted on Formula One's first visit to China, but he was pushed all the way to the flag by Jenson Button, with Kimi Raikkonen also in the mix.

It's hard to know how highly to praise this victory for Rubens Barrichello as it was achieved in a race in which Ferrari team-mate Michael Schumacher drove like a clown in qualifying, a spin leaving him to start from the rear (the pit-lane actually), then performed little better in the race. Still, with his seventh world title in the bag, he could afford these slip-ups. Rubens, meanwhile, could have done no more than he did, claiming pole position and leading the majority of the race for the ninth win of his career.

There was never an idle moment for the Brazilian, though, as Kimi Raikkonen gave chase in his McLaren from the outside of the front row and then Jenson Button hit the front for BAR by dint of staying out several laps longer before making his first pit stop.

But what made the grand prix so compelling was the way that their form kept changing according to the grip offered by their different tyres as both tyre suppliers were found wanting in the compounds that they'd brought for this first visit to this brand-new racing venue. Weirdly, it was as though they'd swapped their regular characteristics, as the Bridgestones would get up to temperature quickly and then lose effectiveness as they grained, with the Michelins doing the reverse as the Bridgestone runners used the Japanese company's softer rubber, the Michelin-shod teams the French firm's harder rubber. This meant, too, that the Bridgestone runners pitted three times, the Michelin men just twice. Which is why the outcome was never going to be known until the final quarter of the race.

It was at this point that it became clear that Barrichello was in control for he was able to emerge from his final pit stop on lap 42 8 seconds clear of Button, with Raikkonen a further 6 seconds back. They concertinaed over the remaining 14 laps, eventually crossing the line with just 1.5 seconds covering them, but Barrichello had matters under control. This is more than can be said of Michael, who was less effective than usual in traffic as he started with a heavy fuel load, then clipped Christian Klien's Jaguar, picked up a puncture and later spun, leaving him a lapped 12th.

Conversely, brother Ralf had shown good speed on his return from injury, outqualifying team-mate Juan Pablo Montoya and leading for a lap, but he was out of sequence and a likely run to fifth or sixth was scuppered when he was torpedoed by Coulthard and caught the team on the hop by pitting just as Montoya came in. He then abandoned his car in a sulk at being asked to pull aside until Montoya's scheduled stop had been completed.

One of the drives of the race came from Takuma Sato who was forced to drop 10 places down the grid after his BAR was given a new Honda V10 for the race, leaving him to fight his way forward from 18th to an eventual sixth.

Ferrari's Rubens Barrichello and McLaren's Kimi Raikkonen whip by the grandstands during their battle for supremacy in the inaugural Chinese Grand Prix

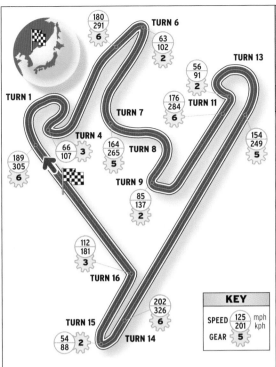

TURN 6
180 / 291 / 6
63 / 102 / 2
TURN 13
56 / 91 / 2
176 / 284 / 6
TURN 11
154 / 249 / 5
TURN 1
TURN 7
TURN 4
66 / 107 / 3
164 / 265 / 5
TURN 8
189 / 305 / 6
TURN 9
85 / 137 / 2
112 / 181 / 3
TURN 16
202 / 326 / 6
TURN 15
54 / 88 / 2
TURN 14

KEY

| SPEED | 125 / 201 | mph / kph |
| GEAR | 5 | |

POLE TIME
Barrichello, 1m34.012s, 129.698mph/208.720kph

WINNER'S AVERAGE SPEED
127.502mph/205.185kph

FASTEST LAP
M Schumacher, 1m32.238s, 132.202mph/212.749kph

LAP LEADERS
Barrichello, 1-12, 16-29, 36-55; Button, 13-14, 30-35; R Schumacher, 15

 SHANGHAI ROUND 16
Date **26 September 2004** Laps **56** Distance **189.68 miles/305.25km**
Weather **Warm, dry and bright**

RACE RESULT

Position	Driver	Team	Result	Stops	Qualifying Time	Grid
1	Rubens Barrichello	Ferrari	1h29m12.420s	3	1m34.012s	1
2	Jenson Button	BAR	1h29m13.455s	2	1m34.295s	3
3	Kimi Raikkonen	McLaren	1h29m13.889s	3	1m34.178s	2
4	Fernando Alonso	Renault	1h29m44.930s	2	1m34.917s	6
5	Juan Pablo Montoya	Williams	1h29m57.613s	2	1m35.245s	10
6	Takuma Sato	BAR	1h30m07.211s	2	1m34.933s	18*
7	Giancarlo Fisichella	Sauber	1h30m17.884s	3	1m34.951s	7
8	Felipe Massa	Sauber	1h30m32.500s	3	1m34.759s	4
9	David Coulthard	McLaren	1h30m33.039s	3	1m35.029s	9
10	Mark Webber	Jaguar	55 laps	2	1m35.286s	11
11	Jacques Villeneuve	Renault	55 laps	2	1m35.384s	12
12	Michael Schumacher	Ferrari	55 laps	3	no time	20
13	Nick Heidfeld	Jordan	55 laps	2	1m36.507s	14
14	Olivier Panis	Toyota	55 laps	3	1m34.975s	8
15	Timo Glock	Jordan	55 laps	2	1m37.140s	16
16	Zsolt Baumgartner	Minardi	53 laps	3	1m40.240s	17
R	Gianmaria Bruni	Minardi	38 laps/lost wheel	2	no time	17
R	Ralf Schumacher	Williams	37 laps/crash damage	2	1m34.891s	5
R	Ricardo Zonta	Toyota	35 laps/gearbox	2	1m35.410s	13
R	Christian Klien	Jaguar	11 laps/crash damage	0	1m36.535s	15

TALKING POINT: JAGUAR SHANGHAIED

Between this grand prix and the previous one, the 500-strong staff of Jaguar Racing had been axed by parent company Ford. A visit to this sparkling new circuit in Shanghai should have brought cheer, but F1 was in a mess, its future confused. FIA President Max Mosley wanted cost-cutting measures to stop teams from folding and to attract new teams in. But the teams weren't playing ball – the only change they wanted was a larger portion of the pie from Bernie Ecclestone. On top of this, the British GP was being threatened with the chop. Happy days…

Christian Klien is pushed into the pit garage during practice

JAPANESE GP

'Rain Stopped Play' wouldn't have been an adequate headline, but Typhoon 22 with its 100mph winds blew past and the Japanese GP took place after all, with Michael Schumacher the only storm in town that day.

There was no doubting who the fans packing the grandstands wanted to win: Takuma Sato. He'd treated them to a fifth place in 2002 with Jordan, then sixth as a late-season stand-in at BAR in 2003. This year, they prayed, he'd be on the podium, perhaps even become the first Japanese driver to win. After all, Honda had promised an uprated engine that would produce close on 1000bhp.

Trouble was, the approach of Typhoon 22 led to Friday's running being held in torrential rain. Saturday was a wash-out. Then, as the wind passed and Sunday morning's rain turned to sunshine, Michael Schumacher took the race by the scruff of the neck and ruled almost as never before. He and his Ferrari were often faster than his closest chaser by more than a second per lap, soon pulling out an unassailable lead.

The early pursuit had come from brother Ralf who was on far better form on his second race back with Williams. But he was the first frontrunner to pit, as early as lap 9. Jenson Button, who'd vaulted past Mark Webber off the line, had run third behind him but had been suffering from oversteer and, to the delight of the crowd, let team-mate Sato by. And this became second after Ralf's pit stop, sending the crowd wild, in a quietly Japanese way.

Michael was already so far clear, though, that it was obvious that he was back at his imperious best and that only misfortune would deny him his 83rd victory. And so it proved, as he revelled in the performance of a new type of Bridgestone tyre and was able to back off and still finish 15 seconds clear.

The only driver who might have stood a chance was Rubens Barrichello, but the stilted matter of qualifying, in their finishing order in China, led to Rubens going out first, and Michael 12th, on a track that was drying fast. This then meant that Michael had the advantage in qualifying proper, going out last but one and nailing pole by half a second over Ralf, with Rubens 14 places behind his team-mate on the grid. Worse still, the new Bridgestones were too soft for a two-stop strategy to help him. But attack he did, rocketing up to sixth place before a lunge at David Coulthard from a long way back into the chicane ended in two cars with suspension askew, both out of the race.

So, Ralf was able to relax and collect second place – his first podium finish of the year – as his three-stop strategy was superior to Button's two-stopper. Sato raced home fourth, troubled in the closing laps by his HANS device slipping, but doing enough to keep Fernando Alonso at bay, with Kimi Rakkonen right behind in sixth.

Of the others, Jacques Villeneuve was off the pace again on his second outing with Renault. While Mark Webber, who had qualified so well for Jaguar, was the first out of the race after something overheated in his cockpit and started burning his behind...

Michael Schumacher leads brother Ralf in a race where they were truly the class of the field

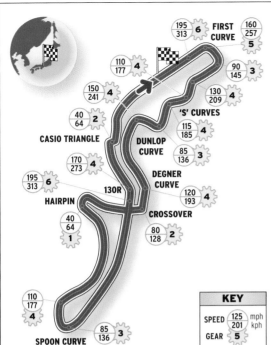

SPEED values on circuit map (mph/kph, gear):
- FIRST CURVE: 195/313 gear 6, 160/257 gear 5
- 110/177 gear 4
- 90/145 gear 3
- 150/241 gear 4
- 130/209 gear 4
- 'S' CURVES: 115/185 gear 4
- 40/64 gear 2
- 85/136 gear 3
- CASIO TRIANGLE
- DUNLOP CURVE
- DEGNER CURVE
- 170/273 gear 4
- 195/313 gear 6
- 130R
- 120/193 gear 4
- HAIRPIN
- CROSSOVER
- 40/64 gear 1
- 80/128 gear 2
- 110/177 gear 4
- 85/136 gear 3
- SPOON CURVE

KEY

SPEED	125 / 201	mph / kph
GEAR	5	

POLE TIME

M Schumacher, 1m33.542s, 138.873mph/223.484kph

WINNER'S AVERAGE SPEED

135.791mph/218.524kph

FASTEST LAP

Barrichello, 1m32.730s, 140.089mph/225.441kph

LAP LEADERS

M Schumacher, 1-53

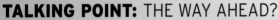

● SUZUKA ROUND 16

Date **10 October 2004** Laps **53** Distance **191.248 miles/307.770km**
Weather **Warm, dry and bright**

RACE RESULT

Position	Driver	Team	Result	Stops	Qualifying Time	Grid
1	Michael Schumacher	Ferrari	1h24m26.985s	3	1m33.542s	1
2	Ralf Schumacher	Williams	1h24m41.083s	3	1m34.032s	2
3	Jenson Button	BAR	1h24m46.647s	2	1m35.157s	5
4	Takuma Sato	BAR	1h24m58.766s	3	1m34.897s	4
5	Fernando Alonso	Renault	1h25m04.752s	2	1m36.663s	11
6	Kimi Raikkonen	McLaren	1h25m06.347s	2	1m36.820s	12
7	Juan Pablo Montoya	Williams	1h25m22.332s	3	1m37.653s	13
8	Giancarlo Fisichella	Sauber	1h25m23.261s	3	1m36.136s	7
9	Felipe Massa	Sauber	1h25m56.641s	3	no time	19
10	Jacques Villeneuve	Renault	52 laps	2	1m36.274s	9
11	Jarno Trulli	Toyota	52 laps	3	1m35.213s	6
12	Christian Klien	Jaguar	52 laps	2	1m38.258s	14
13	Nick Heidfeld	Jordan	52 laps	3	1m41.953s	16
14	Olivier Panis	Toyota	51 laps	3	1m36.420s	10
15	Timo Glock	Jordan	51 laps	3	1m43.533s	17
16	Gianmaria Bruni	Minardi	50 laps	3	48.069s	18
R	Zsolt Baumgartner	Minardi	41 laps/spun off	3	no time	20
R	David Coulthard	McLaren	38 laps/crash	2	1m36.156s	8
R	Rubens Barrichello	Ferrari	38 laps/crash	2	1m38.637s	15
R	Mark Webber	Jaguar	20 laps/discomfort	2	1m34.571s	3

TALKING POINT: THE WAY AHEAD?

Typhoon 22 could have played into FIA President Max Mosley's hands as the way in which the teams coped with the loss of all Saturday running, by transferring pre-qualifying and qualifying to Sunday morning, showed that running a grand prix over two days rather than three could be possible. This could help reduce costs and perhaps give Bernie Ecclestone what he craves: more grands prix in each World Championship. A figure of 20 per year would suit him nicely. Also, for a change, it certainly gave fans something to get excited about on the Sunday morning.

Michael Schumacher kicks up the rain in practice

BRAZILIAN GP

The weekend of the final round was awash with politics as the future format of Formula One was thrashed out,

but there was also a really exciting race, with Juan Pablo Montoya edging out Kimi Raikkonen and Ferrari nowhere.

Rubens Barrichello will wonder what he's ever going to have to do to win his home race. Here he was, starting on pole, racing for the team that had won all but two of the 17 grands prix thus far, with team-mate Michael Schumacher 18th on the 20-car grid after a hefty crash led to him needing to use the T-car and, thus, run a new engine, which meant a ten-place demotion down the grid. Yet, still, he came away without a win at his 12th attempt. Sure, he got to stand on the podium in front of his home crowd for the first time, but he was a crestfallen third, well beaten by both Juan Pablo Montoya and Kimi Raikkonen.

The key to the outcome was the weather, with rain falling briefly 45 minutes before the start of the race. It wasn't much, but it was enough to have the teams debating about whether to send their cars out on wet-weather tyres or to risk putting them on dries. In the end, just three cars went for dries - Fernando Alonso who was eighth on the grid, David Coulthard in 12th and Jacques Villeneuve in 13th. They'd find it tricky to start off, with Alonso running off the track on both the formation lap and the opening lap. However, he was soon the fastest driver out there. Then again, he needed to be, as his Renault dropped to the tail of the field before powering its way back up the order as team chiefs realized that dries were the ones to have and started calling their charges in.

Barrichello had led away, but he was demoted by Raikkonen before the lap was complete. Barrichello then worked his way back to the front as his Bridgestones came up to speed. When he pitted for dries, a lap after most of his rivals, the home crowd had the luxury of seeing another Brazilian driver in the lead: Felipe Massa. He enjoyed the moment, but ought to have pitted earlier, as he ended up in tenth when the order settled down.

Alonso pressed on with his original tyres, leading from the moment Massa pitted on lap 7 until he pitted on lap 18. This seemed to leave him well placed, as he'd be able to pit just once more unless rain fell anew, while his rivals would need to pit twice. Coulthard and Villeneuve would also need to stop once more, but they'd failed to run higher than seventh and eighth.

The main threat to Alonso was clearly going to come from Montoya and Raikkonen, with Montoya taking over the lead in his Williams when Alonso made his first pit stop, from which he emerged sixth.

After Ralf Schumacher, Takuma Sato and Barrichello had all made their second stops, Alonso was back up to third, but it was clear that Montoya or Raikkonen would win. The Finn stayed out for five laps longer before his final stop in an attempt to get ahead of Montoya, but failed, allowing his 2005 team-mate to give Williams the best goodbye present of all.

Alonso's second set of tyres left him understeering and Barrichello claimed third as Alonso did well to keep the three-car pack of Ralf Schumacher, Sato and early spinner Michael Schumacher behind him.

On his home patch, Rubens Barrichello leads at the start, chased by Raikkonen, Massa, Montoya and Button

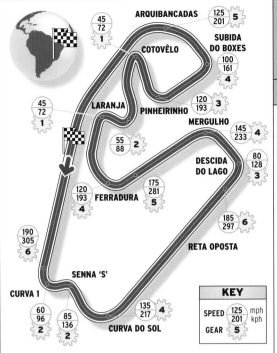

- ARQUIBANCADAS
- 45 / 72 / 1
- 125 / 201 / 5
- COTOVÊLO
- SUBIDA DO BOXES
- 100 / 161 / 4
- 45 / 72 / 1
- LARANJA
- PINHEIRINHO
- 120 / 193 / 3
- MERGULHO
- 55 / 88 / 2
- 145 / 233 / 4
- 80 / 128 / 3
- DESCIDA DO LAGO
- 120 / 193 / 4
- FERRADURA
- 175 / 281 / 5
- 185 / 297 / 6
- 190 / 305 / 6
- RETA OPOSTA
- SENNA 'S'
- CURVA 1
- 60 / 96 / 2
- 85 / 136 / 2
- 135 / 217 / 4
- CURVA DO SOL

KEY

SPEED: 125 mph / 201 kph
GEAR: 5

POLE TIME

Barrichello, 1m10.646s, 136.415mph/219.529kph

WINNER'S AVERAGE SPEED

129.572mph/208.516kph

FASTEST LAP

Montoya, 1m11.473s, 134.867mph/217.038kph

LAP LEADERS

Raikkonen, 1-3, 29, 51-55; Barrichello, 4-5; Massa, 6-7; Alonso, 8-18; Montoya, 19-28, 30-50, 56-71

INTERLAGOS ROUND 18

Date **24 October 2004** Laps **71** Distance **190.067 miles/305.909km**
Weather **Damp, but drying and overcast**

RACE RESULT

Position	Driver	Team	Result	Stops	Qualifying Time	Grid
1	**Juan Pablo Montoya**	Williams	1h28m01.451s	3	1m10.850s	2
2	**Kimi Raikkonen**	McLaren	1h28m02.473s	3	1m10.892s	3
3	**Rubens Barrichello**	Ferrari	1h28m25.550s	3	1m10.646s	1
4	**Fernando Alonso**	Renault	1h28m50.359s	2	1m11.454s	8
5	**Ralf Schumacher**	Williams	1h28m51.191s	3	1m11.131s	7
6	**Takuma Sato**	BAR	1h28m51.699s	3	1m11.120s	6
7	**Michael Schumacher**	Ferrari	1h28m52.077s	3	1m11.386s	18*
8	**Felipe Massa**	Sauber	1h29m03.761s	3	1m10.922s	4
9	**Giancarlo Fisichella**	Sauber	1h29m05.293s	2	1m11.571s	10
10	**Jacques Villeneuve**	Renault	70 laps	2	1m11.836s	13
11	**David Coulthard**	McLaren	70 laps	2	1m11.750s	12
12	**Jarno Trulli**	Toyota	70 laps	3	1m11.483s	9
13	**Ricardo Zonta**	Toyota	70 laps	3	1m11.974s	14
14	**Christian Klien**	Jaguar	69 laps	3	1m12.211s	15
15	**Timo Glock**	Jordan	69 laps	3	1m13.503s	17
16	**Zsolt Baumgartner**	Minardi	67 laps	3	1m13.550s	19
17	**Gianmaria Bruni**	Minardi	67 laps	3	no time	20
R	**Mark Webber**	Jaguar	23 laps/accident	1	1m11.665s	11
R	**Nick Heidfeld**	Jordan	15 laps/clutch	1	1m12.829s	16
R	**Jenson Button**	BAR	3 laps/engine	0	1m11.092s	5

* Demoted ten places for changing engine

TALKING POINT: SERIOUS REVISIONS

The behind-the-scenes action at Interlagos was even more competitive than that on the track. The reason was that the teams were trying to agree on a revision to the 2005 rules that would help them to cut costs, something seen as essential if Jordan and Minardi were not to fold like Jaguar. Among the suggested changes were to limit testing to ten days a year with a pair of free two-hour practice sessions on the Friday of each grand prix meeting. To effect a change, all ten team principals needed to sign the document. Ferrari's Jean Todt refused...

Bernie Ecclestone and Paul Stoddart start getting serious

FINAL RESULTS 2004

	DRIVER	NATIONALITY	ENGINE	Round 1 March 6 AUSTRALIAN GP	Round 2 March 20 MALAYSIAN GP	Round 3 April 3 BAHRAIN GP	Round 4 April 24 SAN MARINO GP	Round 5 May 8 SPANISH GP
1	MICHAEL SCHUMACHER	GER	FERRARI F2004	1PF	1P	1PF	1F	1PF
2	RUBENS BARRICHELLO	BRA	FERRARI F2004	2	4	2	6	2
3	JENSON BUTTON	GBR	BAR-HONDA 006	6	3	3	2P	8
4	FERNANDO ALONSO	SPA	RENAULT R24	3	7	6	4	4
5	JUAN PABLO MONTOYA	COL	WILLIAMS-BMW FW26	5	2F	13	3	R
6	JARNO TRULLI	ITA	RENAULT R24	7	5	4	5	3
			TOYOTA TF104B	-	-	-	-	-
7	KIMI RAIKKONEN	FIN	MCLAREN-MERCEDES MP4-19	R	R	R	8	11
			MCLAREN-MERCEDES MP4-19B	-	-	-	-	-
8	TAKUMA SATO	JAP	BAR-HONDA 006	9	15	5	16	5
9	RALF SCHUMACHER	GER	WILLIAMS-BMW FW26	4	R	7	7	6
10	DAVID COULTHARD	GBR	MCLAREN-MERCEDES MP4-19	8	6	R	12	10
			MCLAREN-MERCEDES MP4-19B	-	-	-	-	-
11	GIANCARLO FISICHELLA	ITA	SAUBER-PETRONAS C23	10	11	11	9	7
12	FELIPE MASSA	BRA	SAUBER-PETRONAS C23	R	8	12	10	9
13	MARK WEBBER	AUS	JAGUAR-COSWORTH R5	R	R	8	13	12
14	OLIVIER PANIS	FRA	TOYOTA TF104	13	12	9	11	R
			TOYOTA TF104B	-	-	-	-	-
15	ANTONIO PIZZONIA	BRA	WILLIAMS-BMW FW26	-	-	-	-	-
16	CHRISTIAN KLIEN	AUT	JAGUAR-COSWORTH R5	11	10	14	14	R
17	CRISTIANO DA MATTA	BRA	TOYOTA TF104	12	9	10	R	13
			TOYOTA TF104B	-	-	-	-	-
18	NICK HEIDFELD	GER	JORDAN-FORD EJ14	R	R	15	R	R
19	TIMO GLOCK	GER	JORDAN-FORD EJ14	-	-	-	-	-
20	ZSOLT BAUMGARTNER	HUN	MINARDI-COSWORTH PS04	R	16	R	15	R
	JACQUES VILLENEUVE	CDN	RENAULT R24	-	-	-	-	-
	RICARDO ZONTA	BRA	TOYOTA TF104B	-	-	-	-	-
	MARC GENE	SPA	WILLIAMS-BMW FW26	-	-	-	-	-
	GIORGIO PANTANO	ITA	JORDAN-FORD EJ14	14	13	16	R	R
	GIANMARIA BRUNI	ITA	MINARDI-COSWORTH PS04	NC	14	17	R	R

SCORING

1st	10 points
2nd	8 points
3rd	6 points
4th	5 points
5th	4 points
6th	3 points
7th	2 points
8th	1 point

CONSTRUCTOR (RACE RESULTS FOR BOTH DRIVERS, IE. FIRST AND SECOND LISTED AS 1/2 WITH

1	FERRARI	1/2	1/4	1/2	1/6	1/2
2	BAR-HONDA	6/9	3/15	3/5	2/16	5/8
3	RENAULT	3/7	5/7	4/6	4/5	3/4
4	WILLIAMS-BMW	4/5	2/R	7/13	3/7	6/R
5	McLAREN-MERCEDES	8/R	6/R	R/R	8/12	10/11
6	SAUBER-PETRONAS	10/R	8/11	11/12	9/10	7/9
7	JAGUAR-COSWORTH	11/R	10/R	8/14	13/14	12/R
8	TOYOTA	12/13	9/12	9/10	11/R	13/R
9	JORDAN-FORD	14/R	13/R	15/16	R/R	R/R
10	MINARDI-COSWORTH	NC/R	14/16	17/R	15/R	R/R

Round 6 May 22 MONACO GP	Round 7 May 29 EUROPEAN GP	Round 8 June 12 CANADIAN GP	Round 9 June 19 UNITED STATES GP	Round 10 July 3 FRENCH GP	Round 11 July 10 BRITISH GP	Round 12 July 24 GERMAN GP	Round 13 August 14 HUNGARIAN GP	Round 14 August 28 BELGIAN GP	Round 15 September 11 ITALIAN GP	Round 16 September 25 CHINESE GP	Round 17 October 9 JAPANESE GP	Round 18 October 23 BRAZILIAN GP	POINTS TOTAL
RF	1PF	1	1	1F	1F	1P	1PF	2	2	12F	1P	7	148
3	2	2F	2PF	3	3	12	2	3	1PF	1P	RF	3P	114
2	3	3	R	5	4	2	5	R	3	2	3	R	85
R	5	R	R	2P	10	3	3	R	R	4	5	4	59
4	8	D	D	8	5	5	4	R	5	5	7	1F	58
1P	4	R	4	4	R	11	R	9P	10	-	-	-	
-	-	-	-	-	-	-	-	-	-	-	11	12	46
R	R	5	6	-	-	-	-	-	-	-	-	-	
-	-	-	-	7	2P	RF	R	1F	R	3	6	2	45
R	R	R	3	R	11	8	6	R	4	6	4	6	34
10	R	DP	R	-	-	-	-	-	-	R	2	5	24
R	R	6	7	-	-	-	-	-	-	-	-	-	
-	-	-	-	6	7	4	9	7	6	9	R	11	24
R	6	4	9	12	6	9	8	5	8	7	8	9	22
5	9	R	R	13	9	13	R	4	12	8	9	8	12
R	7	R	R	9	8	6	10	R	9	10	R	R	7
8	11	D	5	15	R	-	-	-	-	-	-	-	
-	-	-	-	-	-	14	11	8	R	14	14	-	6
-	-	-	-	-	-	7	7	R	7	-	-	-	6
R	12	9	R	11	14	10	13	6	13	R	12	14	3
6	R	D	R	14	13	-	-	-	-	-	-	-	
-	-	-	-	-	-	R	-	-	-	-	-	-	3
7	10	8	R	16	15	R	12	11	14	13	13	R	3
-	-	7	-	-	-	-	-	-	-	15	15	15	2
9	15	10	8	R	R	16	15	R	15	16	R	16	1
-	-	-	-	-	-	-	-	-	-	11	10	10	
-	-	-	-	-	-	-	R	10	11	R	-	13	
-	-	-	-	10	12	-	-	-	-	-	-	-	
R	13	-	R	17	R	15	R	R	R	-	-	-	
R	14	R	R	18	16	17	14	R	R	R	16	17	

TEAM'S BEST RESULT LISTED FIRST)

Round 6 May 22 MONACO GP	Round 7 May 29 EUROPEAN GP	Round 8 June 12 CANADIAN GP	Round 9 June 19 UNITED STATES GP	Round 10 July 3 FRENCH GP	Round 11 July 10 BRITISH GP	Round 12 July 24 GERMAN GP	Round 13 August 14 HUNGARIAN GP	Round 14 August 28 BELGIAN GP	Round 15 September 11 ITALIAN GP	Round 16 September 25 CHINESE GP	Round 17 October 9 JAPANESE GP	Round 18 October 23 BRAZILIAN GP	POINTS TOTAL
3/R	1/2	1/2	1/2	1/3	1/3	1/12	1/2	2/3	1/2	1/12	1/R	3/7	262
2/R	3/R	3/R	3/R	5/R	4/11	2/8	5/6	R/R	3/4	2/6	3/4	6/R	119
1/R	4/5	R/R	4/R	2/4	10/R	3/11	3/R	9/R	10/R	4/11	5/10	4/10	105
4/10	8/R	D/D	R/D	8/10	5/12	5/5	4/7	R/R	5/7	5/R	2/7	1/5	88
R/R	R/R	5/6	6/7	6/7	2/7	4/R	9/R	1/7	6/R	3/9	6/R	2/11	69
5/R	6/9	4/R	9/R	12/13	6/9	9/13	8/R	5/4	8/12	7/8	8/9	8/9	34
R/R	7/12	9/R	R/R	9/11	8/14	6/10	10/13	6/R	9/13	10/R	12/R	14/R	10
6/8	11/R	D/D	5/R	14/15	13/R	14/R	11/R	8/10	11/R	14/R	11/14	12/13	9
7/R	10/13	7/8	R/R	16/17	15/R	15/R	12/R	11/R	14/R	13/15	13/15	15/R	5
9/R	14/15	10/R	8/R	18/R	16/R	16/17	14/15	R/R	15/R	16/R	16/R	16/17	1

F1 RECORDS

GRAND PRIX CHRONOLOGY

1950 The very first FIA World Championship for cars with 1.5-litre supercharged or 4.5-litre normally-aspirated engines. Indianapolis 500 is included as a round, but no F1 teams attend.

1951 BRM and Girling introduce disc brakes.

1952 Championship is run for cars with 2-litre normally aspirated engines, that's to say F2 cars.

1954 Maximum engine capacity increased to 2.5-litres. Supercharged engines are re-admitted if less than 750cc. Minimum race duration of 500km or three hours.

1958 Minimum race duration of 300km or two hours imposed. Vanwall wins first constructors' cup. Moss gets first rear-engined win.

1960 Final win for a rear-engined car. Last year for Indianapolis 500 in championship.

1961 Maximum engine capacity is 1.5-litre normally-aspirated, with a weight limit of 450kg. Commercial fuel becomes mandatory in place of Avgas. Supercharged engines are banned.

1962 Monocoque Lotus revolutionizes F1.

1966 Debut season for 3-litre formula with a 500kg weight limit.

1967 Ford Cosworth DFV, the most successful F1 engine ever, wins on debut. Aerodynamic wings seen for first time above engine.

1968 Wings put on supports to become spoilers, both above front and rear axles. Gold Leaf Lotus heralds age of sponsorship.

1969 Onboard fire extinguishers and roll-hoops made mandatory. Four-wheel drive is toyed with. Moveable aerodynamic devices are banned mid-year.

1970 Bag fuel tanks made mandatory. Minimum weight is 530kg.

1971 Slick tyres are introduced. Lotus tries a gas turbine engine.

1972 Engines with more than 12 cylinders are banned.

1973 Maximum fuel tank size is 250 litres, minimum weight is 575kg. Breathable air driver safety system introduced.

1974 Rear wing overhang limited to 1m behind rear axle.

1975 Hesketh and Hill try carbonfibre aerodynamic parts.

1976 Rear wing overhang cut back to 80cm. Tall air boxes banned from Spanish GP. McLaren introduces Kevlar and Nomex in its structure.

1977 Renault's RS01 brings 1.5-litre turbo engines to F1. Lotus introduces ground effect.

1978 Brabham's "fan car" wins Swedish GP and is banned. Tyrrell tests active suspension.

1979 Renault's Jean-Pierre Jabouille scores first turbo win.

1980 Brabham introduces carbon brake discs.

1981 McLaren's carbonfibre monocoque revolutionizes F1 car construction. Sliding skirts are banned and 6cm ground clearance enforced. Minimum weight now 585kg.

1982 Survival cells made mandatory. Brabham introduces refuelling pit stops.

1983 Brabham's Nelson Piquet and BMW become first turbo world champions. Ground effect is banned and flat bottoms introduced. Michele Alboreto scores last DFV win. Minimum weight cut to 540kg.

1984 Fuel tank cut to 220 litres. Mid-race refuelling banned.

1985 Crash-tested nose box becomes mandatory.

1986 Normally-aspirated engines are banned as F1 goes all-turbo, with maximum fuel capacity of 195 litres.

1987 3.5-litre normally-aspirated engines introduced alongside turbos, with 500kg minimum weight limit against turbos' 540kg. Turbos limited to 4 bar boost.

1988 Pop-off boost limited to 2.5 bar and fuel allowance for turbo cars cut to 150 litres. Drivers' feet must be behind front axle.

1989 Turbo engines banned and fuel tank capacity cut to 150 litres for normally-aspirated engines. Ferrari introduces semi-automatic gearboxes.

1992 Top teams use driver aids such as active suspension, traction control and anti-lock brakes.

1994 Driver aids outlawed. Refuelling pit stops permitted again. Ayrton Senna and Roland Ratzenberger die at Imola, triggering rule changes and introducing more chicanes to slow cars at the faster circuits.

1995 Engine capacity cut. Wing size reduced to cut downforce.

1996 Higher cockpit-side protection made mandatory. Aerodynamic suspension parts banned.

1998 Chassis made narrower. Grooved tyres introduced and slicks banned in order to slow the cars.

1999 Extra groove is added to front and rear tyres.

2001 Traction control is permitted from Spanish GP onwards.

2002 Ferrari dominance spurs FIA to seek solution to make racing more entertaining for 2003.

2003 New 10-8-6-5-4-3-2-1 points system introduced, along with one-at-a-time qualifying procedure and the banning of refuelling between qualifying and the start of the race.

2004 Launch control and fully automatic gearboxes are outlawed. Engines must last an entire grand prix meeting or the driver will be demoted 10 places on the grid.

DRIVERS

Year	Driver	Team
1950	GIUSEPPE FARINA	ALFA ROMEO
1951	JUAN MANUEL FANGIO	ALFA ROMEO (see left)
1952	ALBERTO ASCARI	FERRARI
1953	ALBERTO ASCARI	FERRARI
1954	JUAN MANUEL FANGIO	MASERATI & MERCEDES
1955	JUAN MANUEL FANGIO	MERCEDES
1956	JUAN MANUEL FANGIO	FERRARI
1957	JUAN MANUEL FANGIO	MASERATI
1958	MIKE HAWTHORN	FERRARI
1959	JACK BRABHAM	COOPER
1960	JACK BRABHAM	COOPER
1961	PHIL HILL	FERRARI
1962	GRAHAM HILL	BRM
1963	JIM CLARK	LOTUS
1964	JOHN SURTEES	FERRARI
1965	JIM CLARK	LOTUS
1966	JACK BRABHAM	BRABHAM
1967	DENNY HULME	BRABHAM
1968	GRAHAM HILL	LOTUS
1969	JACKIE STEWART	MATRA
1970	JOCHEN RINDT	LOTUS
1971	JACKIE STEWART	TYRRELL
1972	EMERSON FITTIPALDI	LOTUS
1973	JACKIE STEWART	TYRRELL
1974	EMERSON FITTIPALDI	McLAREN
1975	NIKI LAUDA	FERRARI
1976	JAMES HUNT	McLAREN
1977	NIKI LAUDA	FERRARI
1978	MARIO ANDRETTI	LOTUS
1979	JODY SCHECKTER	FERRARI
1980	ALAN JONES	WILLIAMS
1981	NELSON PIQUET	BRABHAM
1982	KEKE ROSBERG	WILLIAMS
1983	NELSON PIQUET	BRABHAM
1984	NIKI LAUDA	McLAREN
1985	ALAIN PROST	McLAREN
1986	ALAIN PROST	McLAREN
1987	NELSON PIQUET	WILLIAMS
1988	AYRTON SENNA	McLAREN
1989	ALAIN PROST	McLAREN
1990	AYRTON SENNA	McLAREN
1991	AYRTON SENNA	McLAREN
1992	NIGEL MANSELL	WILLIAMS
1993	ALAIN PROST	WILLIAMS
1994	MICHAEL SCHUMACHER	BENETTON
1995	MICHAEL SCHUMACHER	BENETTON
1996	DAMON HILL	WILLIAMS
1997	JACQUES VILLENEUVE	WILLIAMS
1998	MIKA HAKKINEN	McLAREN

DRIVERS (CONT.)

Year	Driver	Team
1999	MIKA HAKKINEN	McLAREN
2000	MICHAEL SCHUMACHER	FERRARI
2001	MICHAEL SCHUMACHER	FERRARI
2002	MICHAEL SCHUMACHER	FERRARI
2003	MICHAEL SCHUMACHER	FERRARI
2004	MICHAEL SCHUMACHER	FERRARI

CONSTRUCTORS

Year	Constructor
1958	Vanwall
1959	Cooper-Climax
1960	Cooper-Climax
1961	Ferrari
1962	BRM
1963	Lotus-Climax
1964	Ferrari
1965	Lotus-Climax
1966	Brabham-Repco
1967	Brabham-Repco
1968	Lotus-Ford DFV
1969	Matra-Ford DFV
1970	Lotus-Ford DFV
1971	Tyrrell-Ford DFV
1972	Lotus-Ford DFV
1973	Lotus-Ford DFV
1974	McLaren-Ford DFV
1975	Ferrari
1976	Ferrari
1977	Ferrari

CONSTRUCTORS (CONT.)

Year	Constructor
1978	Lotus-Ford DFV
1979	Ferrari
1980	Williams-Ford DFV
1981	Williams-Ford DFV
1982	Ferrari
1983	Ferrari
1984	McLaren-TAG
1985	McLaren-TAG
1986	Williams-Honda
1987	Williams-Honda
1988	McLaren-Honda
1989	McLaren-Honda
1990	McLaren-Honda
1991	McLaren-Honda
1992	Williams-Renault
1993	Williams-Renault
1994	Williams-Renault
1995	Benetton-Renault
1996	Williams-Renault
1997	Williams-Renault
1998	McLaren-Mercedes
1999	Ferrari
2000	Ferrari
2001	Ferrari
2002	Ferrari
2003	Ferrari
2004	Ferrari

Lotus ace Jim Clark was the first British driver to become a multiple World Champion

MOST GRANDS PRIX STARTS

DRIVERS

256	Riccardo Patrese ITA	149	Rene Arnoux FRA
213	Michael Schumacher GER	147	Eddie Irvine GBR,
210	Gerhard Berger AUT		Derek Warwick GBR
208	Andrea de Cesaris ITA	146	Carlos Reutemann ARG
204	Nelson Piquet BRA	144	Emerson Fittipaldi BRA
201	Jean Alesi FRA	135	Jean-Pierre Jarier FRA
199	Alain Prost FRA	134	Jacques Villeneuve CDN
198	Rubens Barrichello BRA	132	Eddie Cheever USA,
194	Michele Alboreto ITA		Clay Regazzoni SUI
187	Nigel Mansell GBR	130	Jarno Trulli ITA
176	Graham Hill GBR	128	Mario Andretti USA
175	David Coulthard GBR,	127	Ralf Schumacher GER
	Jacques Laffite FRA	126	Jack Brabham AUS
171	Niki Lauda AUT	124	Giancarlo Fisichella ITA
163	Thierry Boutsen BEL	123	Ronnie Peterson SWE
162	Mika Hakkinen FIN,	119	Pierluigi Martini ITA
	Johnny Herbert GBR	116	Damon Hill GBR,
161	Ayrton Senna BRA		Jacky Ickx BEL,
159	Heinz-Harald Frentzen GER		Alan Jones AUS
158	Martin Brundle GBR,	114	Keke Rosberg FIN,
	Olivier Panis FRA		Patrick Tambay FRA
152	John Watson GBR		

CONSTRUCTORS

704	Ferrari	394	Brabham	198	Sauber
577	McLaren	383	Arrows	197	BRM
496	Williams	322	Minardi	174	Renault
490	Lotus	317	Benetton	134	Jaguar
418	Tyrrell	231	Jordan	132	Osella
409	Prost	230	March	129	Cooper

MOST GRANDS PRIX WINS

DRIVERS

83	Michael Schumacher GER		Alan Jones AUS,
51	Alain Prost FRA		Carlos Reutemann ARG
41	Ayrton Senna BRA	11	Jacques Villeneuve CDN
31	Nigel Mansell GBR	10	Gerhard Berger AUT,
27	Jackie Stewart GBR		James Hunt GBR,
25	Jim Clark GBR,		Ronnie Peterson SWE,
	Niki Lauda AUT		Jody Scheckter RSA
24	Juan Manuel Fangio ARG	9	Rubens Barrichello BRA
23	Nelson Piquet BRA	8	Denny Hulme NZL,
22	Damon Hill GBR		Jacky Ickx BEL
20	Mika Hakkinen FIN	7	Rene Arnoux FRA
16	Stirling Moss GBR	6	Tony Brooks GBR,
14	Jack Brabham AUS,		Jacques Laffite FRA,
	Emerson Fittipaldi BRA,		Riccardo Patrese FRA,
	Graham Hill GBR		Jochen Rindt AUT,
13	Alberto Ascari ITA,		Ralf Schumacher GER,
	David Coulthard GBR		John Surtees GBR,
12	Mario Andretti USA,		Gilles Villeneuve CDN

CONSTRUCTORS

182	Ferrari	10	Alfa Romeo	1	Eagle,
138	McLaren	9	Ligier,		Hesketh,
112	Williams		Maserati,		Penske,
79	Lotus		Matra,		Porsche,
35	Brabham		Mercedes,		Shadow,
27	Benetton		Vanwall		Stewart
23	Tyrrell	4	Jordan		
17	BRM,	3	March,		
	Renault		Wolf		
16	Cooper	2	Honda		

Alain Prost became very accustomed to spraying the bubbly, winning 51 times. This is at the Brazilian Grand Prix in 1988

Alberto Ascari after winning the 1953 British Grand Prix at Silverstone

MOST CONSECUTIVE WINS

DRIVERS

9	Alberto Ascari ITA 1952–53	Damon Hill GBR 1995,
7	Michael Schumacher GER 2004	Damon Hill GBR 1996,
6	Michael Schumacher GER 2000	Alain Prost FRA 1993,
	Michael Schumacher GER 2001	Jochen Rindt AUT 1970,
5	Jack Brabham AUS 1960,	Michael Schumacher GER 1994,
	Jim Clark GBR 1965,	Michael Schumacher GER 2002,
	Nigel Mansell GBR 1992,	Ayrton Senna BRA 1988,
	Michael Schumacher GER 2004	Ayrton Senna BRA 1991
4	Jack Brabham AUS 1966,	
	Jim Clark GBR 1963,	
	Juan Manuel Fangio ARG 1953,	
	Juan Manuel Fangio ARG 1954,	

MOST WINS IN ONE SEASON

DRIVERS

13	Michael Schumacher GER 2004	Ayrton Senna BRA 1991,
11	Michael Schumacher GER 2002	Jacques Villeneuve CDN 1997
9	Nigel Mansell GBR 1992,	6 Mario Andretti USA 1978,
	Michael Schumacher GER 1995,	Alberto Ascari ITA 1952,
	Michael Schumacher GER 2000,	Jim Clark GBR 1965,
	Michael Schumacher GER 2001	Juan Manuel Fangio ARG 1954,
8	Mika Hakkinen FIN 1998,	Damon Hill GBR 1994,
	Damon Hill GBR 1996,	James Hunt GBR 1976,
	Michael Schumacher GER 1994,	Nigel Mansell GBR 1987,
	Ayrton Senna BRA 1988	Michael Schumacher GER 1998,
7	Jim Clark GBR 1963,	Michael Schumacher GER 2003,
	Alain Prost FRA 1984,	Ayrton Senna BRA 1989,
	Alain Prost FRA 1988,	Ayrton Senna BRA 1990
	Alain Prost FRA 1993,	

CONSTRUCTORS

15	Ferrari 2004,	Lotus 1978,	Ferrari 1976,
	Ferrari 2002,	McLaren 1991,	Ferrari 1979,
	McLaren 1988	Williams 1997	Ferrari 1990,
12	McLaren 1984,	7 Ferrari 1952,	Ferrari 1996,
	Williams 1996	Ferrari 1953,	Ferrari 1998,
11	Benetton 1995	Lotus 1963,	Ferrari 1999,
10	Ferrari 2000,	Lotus 1973,	Lotus 1965,
	McLaren 1989,	McLaren 1999,	Lotus 1970,
	Williams 1992,	McLaren 2000,	Matra 1969 ,
	Williams 1993	Tyrrell 1971,	McLaren 1976,
9	Ferrari 2001,	Williams 1991,	McLaren 1985,
	McLaren 1998,	Williams 1994	McLaren 1990,
	Williams 1986,	6 Alfa Romeo 1950,	Vanwall 1958,
	Williams 1987	Alfa Romeo 1951,	Williams 1980
8	Benetton 1994,	Cooper 1960,	
	Ferrari 2003,	Ferrari 1975,	

STARTS WITHOUT A WIN

DRIVERS

208	Andrea de Cesaris ITA	99	Pedro Diniz BRA
158	Martin Bundle GBR	97	Chris Amon NZL
147	Derek Warwick GBR	95	Ukyo Katayama JAP
135	Jean-Pierre Jarier FRA	93	Ivan Capelli ITA
132	Eddie Cheever USA	85	Nick Heidfeld GER
119	Pierluigi Martini ITA	84	Jenson Button GBR,
111	Mika Salo FIN		Jonathan Palmer GBR
109	Philippe Alliot FRA	82	Marc Surer SUI
107	Jos Verstappen NED	79	Stefan Johansson SWE

Ayrton Senna won six times in 1989 but still lost out to team-mate Alain Prost

Nigel Mansell was champion in 1992 before coming back, briefly, for more in 1994

MOST POLE POSITIONS

DRIVERS - TOTAL

65	Ayrton Senna BRA		17	Jackie Stewart GBR
63	Michael Schumacher GER		16	Stirling Moss GBR
33	Jim Clark GBR, Alain Prost FRA		14	Alberto Ascari ITA, James Hunt GBR, Ronnie Peterson SWE
32	Nigel Mansell GBR		13	Rubens Barrichello BRA, Jack Brabham AUS, Graham Hill GBR, Jacky Ickx BEL, Jacques Villeneuve CDN
29	Juan Manuel Fangio ARG			
26	Mika Hakkinen FIN			
24	Niki Lauda AUT, Nelson Piquet BRA			
20	Damon Hill GBR		12	Gerhard Berger AUT, David Coulthard GBR
18	Mario Andretti USA, Rene Arnoux FRA			

CONSTRUCTORS - TOTAL

178	Ferrari	14	Tyrrell	7	Vanwall
124	Williams	12	Alfa Romeo	5	March
115	McLaren	11	BRM, Cooper	4	Matra
107	Lotus			3	Shadow
39	Brabham	10	Maserati	2	Jordan, Lancia
36	Renault	9	Prost		
16	Benetton	8	Mercedes	1	BAR, Jaguar

DRIVERS - IN ONE SEASON

14	Nigel Mansell GBR 1992		Michael Schumacher GER 2000
13	Alain Prost FRA 1993, Ayrton Senna BRA 1988, Ayrton Senna BRA 1989		
11	Mika Hakkinen FIN 1999, Michael Schumacher GER 2001	8	Mario Andretti USA 1978, James Hunt GBR 1976, Nigel Mansell GBR 1987, Michael Schumacher GER 2004, Ayrton Senna BRA 1986, Ayrton Senna BRA 1991
10	Ayrton Senna BRA 1990, Jacques Villeneuve CDN 1997		
9	Mika Hakkinen FIN 1998, Damon Hill GBR 1996, Niki Lauda AUT 1974, Niki Lauda AUT 1975, Ronnie Peterson SWE 1973, Nelson Piquet BRA 1984,	7	Mario Andretti USA 1977, Jim Clark GBR 1963, Damon Hill GBR 1995, JP Montoya COL 2002, M Schumacher GER 2002, Ayrton Senna BRA 1985

CONSTRUCTORS - IN ONE SEASON

15	McLaren 1988, McLaren 1989, Williams 1992, Williams 1993		Williams 1995, Williams 1996		McLaren 1991, Renault 1982
12	Ferrari 2004, Lotus 1978, McLaren 1990, McLaren 1998, Williams 1987,	11	Ferrari 2001, McLaren 1999, Williams 1997	9	Brabham 1984, Ferrari 1975
		10	Ferrari 1974, Ferrari 2000, Ferrari 2002, Lotus 1973,		

MOST FASTEST LAPS

DRIVERS

65	Michael Schumacher GER		18	David Coulthard GBR
41	Alain Prost FRA		15	Rubens Barrichello BRA, Clay Regazzoni SUI, Jackie Stewart GBR
30	Nigel Mansell GBR			
28	Jim Clark GBR			
25	Mika Hakkinen FIN		14	Jacky Ickx BEL
24	Niki Lauda AUT		13	Alberto Ascari ITA, Alan Jones AUS, Riccardo Patrese ITA
23	Juan Manuel Fangio ARG, Nelson Piquet BRA			
21	Gerhard Berger AUT		12	Rene Arnoux FRA, Jack Brabham AUS
19	Damon Hill GBR, Stirling Moss GBR, Ayrton Senna BRA		11	Juan Pablo Montoya COL, John Surtees GBR

CONSTRUCTORS

180	Ferrari	20	Tyrrell	12	Matra
128	Williams	19	Renault	11	Prost
114	McLaren	15	BRM, Maserati	9	Mercedes
71	Lotus			7	March
40	Brabham	14	Alfa Romeo	6	Vanwall
35	Benetton	13	Cooper		

Michael Schumacher is now out in front, with his 2003 drivers' title – his sixth – outstripping Juan Manuel Fangio's record of five which had stood since the 1950s

MOST POINTS

This figure is the gross tally, i.e. includes scores that were later dropped

DRIVERS

1186	Michael Schumacher GER	**310**	Carlos Reutemann ARG
798.5	Alain Prost FRA	**289**	Graham Hill GBR
614	Ayrton Senna BRA	**281**	Emerson Fittipaldi BRA,
485.5	Nelson Piquet BRA		Riccardo Patrese ITA
482	Nigel Mansell GBR	**277.5**	Juan Manuel Fangio ARG
475	David Coulthard GBR	**274**	Jim Clark GBR
451	Rubens Barrichello BRA	**261**	Jack Brabham AUS
420.5	Niki Lauda AUT	**259**	Ralf Schumacher GER
420	Mika Hakkinen FIN	**255**	Jody Scheckter RSA
385	Gerhard Berger AUT	**248**	Denny Hulme NZL
360	Damon Hill GBR,	**242**	Jean Alesi FRA
	Jackie Stewart GBR		

CONSTRUCTORS

3344.5	Ferrari	**424**	Prost	**79**	Wolf
2858.5	McLaren	**333**	Cooper	**67.5**	Shadow
2435.5	Williams	**275**	Jordan	**57**	Vanwall
1352	Lotus	**182**	BAR	**54**	Surtees
877.5	Benetton	**176**	Sauber		
854	Brabham	**171.5**	March		
617	Tyrrell	**167**	Arrows		
528	Renault	**155**	Matra		
439	BRM	**88**	Jaguar		

MOST TITLES

DRIVERS

7	Michael Schumacher GER	**1**	Mario Andretti USA,
5	Juan Manuel Fangio ARG		Giuseppe Farina ITA,
4	Alain Prost FRA		Mike Hawthorn GBR,
3	Jack Brabham AUS,		Damon Hill GBR,
	Niki Lauda AUT,		Phil Hill USA,
	Nelson Piquet BRA,		Denis Hulme NZL,
	Ayrton Senna BRA,		James Hunt GBR,
	Jackie Stewart GBR		Alan Jones AUS,
2	Alberto Ascari ITA,		Nigel Mansell GBR,
	Jim Clark GBR,		Jochen Rindt AUT,
	Emerson Fittipaldi BRA,		Keke Rosberg FIN,
	Mika Hakkinen FIN,		Jody Scheckter RSA,
	Graham Hill GBR		John Surtees GBR,
			Jacques Villeneuve CDN

CONSTRUCTORS

14	Ferrari	**2**	Brabham,		Matra,
9	Williams		Cooper		Tyrrell,
8	McLaren	**1**	Benetton,		Vanwall
7	Lotus		BRM,		

2005 FILL IN CHART

DRIVER	TEAM	Round 1 March 6 AUSTRALIAN GP	Round 2 March 20 MALAYSIAN GP	Round 3 April 3 BAHRAIN GP	Round 4 April 24 SAN MARINO GP	Round 5 May 8 SPANISH GP	Round 6 May 22 MONACO GP	Round 7 May 29 EUROPEAN GP
1 MICHAEL SCHUMACHER	FERRARI							
2 RUBENS BARRICHELLO	FERRARI							
3 JENSON BUTTON	BAR							
4 TAKUMA SATO	BAR							
5 FERNANDO ALONSO	RENAULT							
6 GIANCARLO FISICHELLA	RENAULT							
7 MARK WEBBER	WILLIAMS							
8 ANTONIO PIZZONIA (TBC)	WILLIAMS							
9 KIMI RAIKKONEN	MCLAREN							
10 JUAN PABLO MONTOYA	MCLAREN							
11 FELIPE MASSA	SAUBER							
12 JACQUES VILLENEUVE	SAUBER							
13 DAVID COULTHARD	RED BULL							
14 CHRISTIAN KLIEN (TBC)	RED BULL							
15 RALF SCHUMACHER	TOYOTA							
16 JARNO TRULLI	TOYOTA							
17 ROBERT DOORNBOOS	JORDAN							
18 TBA	JORDAN							
19 CHRISTIJAN ALBERS	MINARDI							
20 TBA	MINARDI							

Round 8 June 12 CANADIAN GP	**Round 9** June 19 UNITED STATES GP	**Round 10** July 3 FRENCH GP	**Round 11** July 10 BRITISH GP	**Round 12** July 24 GERMAN GP	**Round 13** July 31 HUNGARIAN GP	**Round 14** August 21 TURKISH GP	**Round 15** September 4 ITALIAN GP	**Round 16** September 11 BELGIAN GP	**Round 17** September 25 BRAZILIAN GP	**Round 18** October 9 JAPANESE GP	**Round 19** October 16 CHINESE GP	**POINTS TOTAL**

SCORING SYSTEM: 10, 8, 6, 5, 4, 3, 2, 1 POINTS FOR THE FIRST EIGHT FINISHERS IN EACH RACE

The publishers would like to thanks the following sources for their kind permission to reproduce the pictures in this book. The page numbers for each of the photographs are listed below, giving the page on which they appear in the book. Any location indicator (c-centre, t-top, b-bottom, l-left, r-right)

Corbis: /Stringer: 67
Empics: /James Bearne: 21; /Miaomiao: 12
Getty Images: /AFP: 8; /Torsten Blackwood: 26, 30; /Marcus Brandt: 50; /Simon Bruty: 106; /Denis Charlet: 92; /Stanley Chou: 29; /Robert Cianflone: 44; /Paolo Cocco: 47; /Express: 107t; /Fox Photos: 405; /Jean-Loup Gautreau: 73, 74, 64-65; /Paul Gilham: 17, 33t, 69; /Patrick Hertzog: 19; /Mike Hewitt: 108; /Liu Jin: 96, 42-43; /Keystone: 104; /Attila Kisbenedek: 90; /Robert Laberge: 51; /Bryn Lennon: 16, 54, 58, 62, 97, 100; /Clive Mason: 46; /Peter Parks: 20; /Pool: 11; /Mike Powell: 112; /Pascal Rondeau: 107b; /Clive Rose: 2, 9, 18, 25, 28, 35b, 36, 52, 76, 88, 91, 94, 109; /Mark Thompson: 6-7 10, 14, 15, 22, 23, 24, 27, 32, 33b, 34, 36, 41, 45, 48, 60, 63, 79, 95, 98, 101; /Yoshikazu Tsuno: 31, 35t; /Greg Wood: 66; /Toru Yamanaka: 99
LAT Photographic: 4-5, 49, 82, 84, 86, 87; /Charles Coates: 55, 56, 72, 77; /Julien Crosnier: 85; /Martyn Elford: 40; /Steve Etherington: 68, 75, 78, 80, 81, 83, 89, 93; /Spinney: 37; /Steven Tee: 71
Sporting Pictures: 57, 59; /Crispin Thruston: 53, 61
Sutton Motorsport: /World©Moy: 39; ©World: 13

Illustrations: **Graphic News**

Every effort has been made to acknowledge correctly and contact the source and/or copyright holder of each picture and Carlton Books Limited apologises for any unintentional errors or omissions that will be corrected in future editions of this book.